You Always Call Me Princess

Yvonne,

We hope you enjoy reading about Shellie's exceptional life that was made possible by great friends, teachers & neighbors.

Sincerely
Ted

A True Story

Where acceptance and inculsion triumphs over disabilities

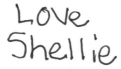

Love
Shellie

David Ted Eyre

You Always Call Me Princess

A True Story

You Always Call Me Princess copyright © 2008 by David Ted Eyre

Published and Distributed by:

GRANITE PUBLISHING AND DISTRIBUTION, LLC
868 NORTH 1430 WEST
OREM, UT. 84057
(801) 229-9023   TOLL FREE (800) 574-5779
FAX (801) 229-1924

Interior Design by
TriQuest Book Services
Orem, Utah

Published in the United States of America

To All Celestial Children
&
To Those Who's Privilege it is to Raise Them

CONTENTS

Preface

One of the greatest privileges in life is to be taught by individuals who have knowledge, understanding, and insight. I have had that blessing many times in my life. However, in the case of this story, the fundamental role of the parent teaching the child was reversed.

When our oldest daughter Shellie entered our lives, we were overwhelmed with our perceived inadequacies of raising a child with disabilities. The unexpected urgency of the moment often makes it difficult to understand that, what may first be viewed as a tragic situation, could turn into one of life's greatest blessings.

This is a story of such a journey. Although it is told only through the eyes of a father, it is an adventure that involved a complete family, then a school system, and eventually an entire community. It is a message of hope, love, acceptance, and inclusion.

For those who have felt the exhilaration of climbing to a mountaintop, they realize that the magnificent vistas that now lay before them were only made possible by the success of each challenging upward step. Shellie's life story, and its message of faith, can be more greatly appreciated by sharing many of the footprints made along the way. I hope you enjoy the inspirational assent that has made up her life.

Ted Eyre
Murray, Utah

ONE

A Casual Hello

If your concentration was keen and your eyes were sharp, you could make out the silhouette of the Grumman Goose long before you would hear the drone of the twin radial engines. Jerry Gatewood and I stood on the end of the pier and stared across the channel towards the southern coast of California. Knowing this flight was coming from Long Beach, our focus was to the south of what it would have been had the plane departed from San Pedro. Countless times we had engaged in a contest to see who could spot the aircraft first, and countless times I had lost. Each time it worried and bothered me more.

"There it is," Jerry asserted with an arrogant tone, knowing he had defeated me once again. Why did I continue to indulge him in this ludicrous game anyway? I stood there quietly, staring at the object of our focus as it grew slowly larger, and before we could hear the engines, I turned to walk down the steep ramp which led to the small floating dock below.

The course of the aircraft's descent continued without the smallest measure of variance until just before it was to touch down. Then, just a few feet above the water, the nose pitched up one or two degrees to lessen the slope and heighten the anticipation of the impending contact with the calm waters of the Avalon Harbor. After one small bounce, the craft settled into a wake of white foam surrounded by the calm, bluish green environment it had just disturbed. Now it was less of an airplane and more of an aquatic bird. As it continued to taxi towards the pier, the dock we were standing on began to rhythmically undulate below us. Jerry and I looked toward each other, with an equivalent grin, to assure the other that this had in no way disturbed our balance. The blue and white vintage aircraft, with the words Catalina Airlines written along its fuselage, made a wide sweeping 180-degree turn in the harbor to align itself for a gentle union with our floating platform.

Jerry had the bow rope ready and I ducked under the passing wing in order to secure the tail of the aircraft to the dock. Our relative positions dictated whose turn it was to unload either passengers or baggage. With the airplane now tightly anchored, Jerry reached for the handle on the side of the bow, just forward of the windshield, and I reached for the one on the rear door. In an unplanned simultaneous motion, both doors were opened to allow access to the forward baggage and rear passenger compartments. As Jerry reached inside the unlatched portal, I secured the door to the side of the plane and positioned myself to help the passenger through the small and awkward opening. After flying through the air, bouncing on the water, and now trying to gain their balance on a floating dock, the new arrivals seemed to be in a rush to get back to solid ground. One by one I would grab a hand and sometimes reach behind an elbow in order to aid their egress from the aircraft, while at the same time welcoming them to Avalon with calm assurance. First came an older couple, then the typical young honeymooners, next a businessman, followed by a young teenage girl with a slightly older female companion, and last, an elementary school-aged boy who I recognized as being a local. This passenger load made for an almost full airplane.

By the time I reached the bow, Jerry had nearly all the baggage and freight unloaded. As he reached in for the last large cardboard box of fresh lettuce, he couldn't help but inquire, "Any keepers?" It was a familiar request, met with a characteristic reply.

"Well, the range was somewhere between 15 and 50, which I know is well within your standards, and with only three suitcases which probably belong to the newlyweds, the rest all look like 'day trippers.' Looks like it's going to be another lonely night in paradise."

"The trouble with you, Ted, is that you're just not naturally optimistic. We still have four more planes today. Still plenty of time to get lucky." I neither smiled nor chose to endorse his bright outlook, but merely tilted my head back as if to point with my chin toward the large, round aluminum canisters next to Jerry's feet.

"What's the movie of the week?" I asked. He lifted the metal containers about chest high, and then, leaning his head back as if to look through some invisible bifocals, he elongated the first word of the title.

"So-o-u-u-th Pacific. What an appropriate flick for our little tropical island. You going to troll the beach front for some hapless tourist, or try an' scare up a local?" he inquired.

"I can't afford to go myself, never mind entertain a date."

With sincere optimism, he replied, "Ah, me boy, where there's a will, there's always a way."

By this time, I had one small bag under my armpit and one larger bag in each hand. Jerry had stacked two cardboard boxes of produce on top of each other and we were making our way up the ramp. From there we would proceed down to the shore end of the pier where we had a small office. One more trip each, then we would load up whatever departing passengers there were and untie the airplane. As the engines came up to takeoff power, we walked back towards the office without even watching the noisy boat evolve back into an airplane.

Once at the office, we divided up what needed to be delivered. Jerry placed all the cartons of produce that he would be taking to the local restaurants through the side door of the Volkswagen van as I put the film canisters in the wire basket of our company bicycle. He then proceeded up Catalina Avenue to the various businesses as I peddled along the beach-front road towards the large round building called the Casino. This was where the only theater in town was located. I always liked coming to the Casino. It was a very high, large round building and was once a great ballroom for dancing during the big band era. I could close my eyes and just imagine the couples, dressed up in their finest evening attire, dancing to the songs of Tommy Dorsey or Glenn Miller. I could visualize my parents dancing in there as they had on one of their first dates in a similar ball room at Salt Air on the southern shore of the Great Salt Lake. How easily it must have been for them to fall in love with each other in such a romantic environment. The days of the big bands were now gone, but fortunately, the love my mother and father shared with each other was not.

I knocked on the locked outer door of the office of the theater. A man in his mid forties answered the door and I handed him the film canisters. I had learned from previous experience that there was no need to make light conversation. Even when he said "Thank you," you knew he really didn't mean it.

Returning to the bike, which I had leaned against one of the palm trees surrounding the Casino, I paused to look at the beautiful beach as it arched its way back towards the pier. There were just a handful of people on the beach this time of the morning, but about 200 yards away, I could see two young children running back and forth as they teased the small waves that were breaking on the beach before retreating back to the ocean. What a change of scenery this was for a boy from Cheyenne, Wyoming. Palm trees had replaced pine trees, a breeze had replaced wind, and an ocean beach had replaced drifting snow.

I slowly peddled my way back along the beach-front until I had come about half the distance to the pier. There, I stopped and leaned the bike up against the wall that separated the walkway from the beach. As I looked up the street that led away from the boardwalk, I saw the Volkswagen van turning the corner at the end of the block. Jerry had probably made his last delivery and was returning to the office at the foot of the pier. About three businesses up the street, on the right side, just past the grocery store, was the post office. There was no mail service in this one-square-mile town and hardly even a need for post office boxes. General delivery would normally suffice. We had provided the post office with the only supply of mail it would receive today from our early morning flight, and I knew by now they would have it sorted. I had my fingers crossed on both hands in hopes that there would be a letter for me today. I could visualize a long message from my mother, expanding on everything that was happening with the rest of my family, along with a complete explanation of the past week's weather, and ending with questions about my general health and eating habits. Then, like always, my dad would add just one or two lines, confirming and verifying everything mom had said.

By the time this daydream was almost complete, I found myself turning into the post office and was nearly at the counter. Even though the request was always the same, each day I tried to word it a little differently. "Anything with my name on it today?" I asked. As the small, kindhearted woman began to search through the stack of unopened envelopes, I was reminded of the irony that existed here. I had always been too shy to ask her what her name was, and yet she must have known the name of every person living on the entire island.

"There is," she replied, "and it looks rather official." This wasn't the letter I had hoped for. My steps were much slower as I walked towards the open door.

Departing the post office, I turned to the left and started down the street towards the bike. I took only a few steps before I stopped, stared at the front of the envelope, and slowly opened it. The one page letter was neatly typed and had a very impressive and official letterhead. The opening line read, "Greetings from the President of the United States." While my head was slowly lowering to look down at the sidewalk below, I could feel a long slow breath being released. I closed my eyes and thought, *"Well, if they have gone to all the trouble to find me on this tiny island, they can have me."*

The hand I had held just a few minutes ago as I helped the young girl from the airplane, the hand which years from today I would place a ring on, was now rummaging through a purse to locate a few coins with which to pay for the postcards she had selected. What different and divergent courses our lives would take before our paths would cross again and I would embrace her in my arms as my wife. A year from today, she would be but one year closer to her high school graduation. A year from today, I would be standing on another beach with another envelope in my hand. The sender of the envelope would be the same, but this one would be larger and light brown in color. Inside it would be orders instructing me on how to report to a place called Long Thon North. The familiar sound of those vintage radial engines I was used to now, would be replaced with the roar of jet engines, as a flight of two heavily laden F-4 Phantoms rolled down the runway in full afterburner. I would turn away from the noise to see a sign, hastily painted on a board above the doorway leading into a large, dark green tent. With sarcastic irony it read, "Welcome to Vietnam."

TWO

The Cycles of Growth

By necessity, my adjustment to the conditions and attitudes surrounding me in Southeast Asia were made swift. By contrast, my reorientation to the country I called home would take much longer. Physically and historically, the war was now far behind both our country and myself. Mentally and emotionally, it would endure much longer for both of us.

For the next two years, I withdrew to the mountains of Colorado where I could broaden my knowledge of construction and renew my affair with skiing. What initially must have drawn me there was the stark contrast between everything I wanted to renew and everything I wanted to forget. The memory of the sweltering jungle was now replaced with snow-covered mountains. The fear of the enemy was supplanted by the gaiety of family and friends.

Renewed both emotionally and financially, I was now in a position to return to California where I could resume my flying. What guided me to a town across the bay from San Francisco, and what led me to people who would alter my life forever, I now believe, was the same power that took the time to hear a child's prayer or to create a universe. Over the past few years, I had allowed a void to develop within me, where I either dismissed or ignored the fact that such a force existed. Events would soon come into place where I would need that assurance more than ever.

I had grossly underestimated the amount of money I would need to sustain myself while going to school. Fortunately, I was able to obtain employment at an aluminum foundry within bicycle range of my apartment. The swing shift offered me both time for school and for work. It was assembly line work that was interesting at first, but soon grew very tedious. We seldom, if ever, saw the office personnel, but the people whom I spent my evenings with were a wonderful cross section of the American working class. Spanish-Americans, Afro-Americans, Native-Americans, and Americans without hyphens stood behind the huge band saws and grinding machines. Hot molten metal was poured into the line of black sand moldings by men with as much sweat on their shoulders as there was on their foreheads.

The night foreman and I became friends quickly, which was much more common for him than it was for myself. In his late 20's, Jerry Guffy stood over 6 feet 3 inches, with a slender build and a personality that was much more comfortable in cowboy boots than tennis shoes. His Missouri accent was accompanied by an ever-present smile and eyes that conveyed a continual and charming sense of mischievousness. His preoccupation with what he considered the most fundamental concern in life led most of our conversations to be centered around members of the opposite sex. Constantly addressing me in our conversations by reference to my last name, he approached me one Thursday morning towards the end of our shift. "Eyre, have I got a deal for you! I've been datin' this girl by the name of Sharon Spencer for a long time now. She has this here roommate that would make a bulldog break his chain. How about the two of us making it an evening with the two of them tomorrow night?" As I tried to correlate all the excuses running through my head as quickly as possible, I could tell that anyone as honest as Jerry could discern a lie a mile away.

"Thanks, Jerry, but the last thing I want is a blind date." His reply was too quick for an appropriate counter.

"Oh, you'll be thankin' me a lot, because this girl might be the last date you ever want." The courtship lasted three years, but the feelings Jerry expressed that night would prove to be wonderfully prophetic.

Ruth Peters was the last of four children, interestingly the same position I held in our family. She had dark brown shoulder length hair with red highlights that surrounded a beautiful countenance which captured your heart as quickly as it did your eyes. Her radiant smile disclosed her thoughts, but it was through her dazzling eyes that you could see into her heart. What different, but augmenting attributes we each brought into the relationship. I brought experience; she brought fidelity. I brought awareness; she brought integrity. I brought an accepting nature; she brought sincerity. I could only hope that everything she was, I could become.

I was 30 years old when we were married and had been on several different continents. I had done and seen many things by myself, and I now knew I never wanted to be alone again.

The cycles of growth have always amazed me. When I was in my teens, I believed I would come to understand it all in my twenties. Now in my thirties, with a child on the way and uncertain employment, I realized just how little I knew and how much I had yet to learn. What makes these experiences exciting and rewarding is when you can share them with someone you love and trust. Ruth had become more beautiful to me every year we had been together, and now the glow of expectant motherhood made her face even more radiant.

The birth of a wonderfully healthy baby boy brought a completeness to our marriage that neither of us had imagined before. We had gone from being husband and wife to being a mother and father. Instead of being a couple, we were now a family. We had entered a new era in our lives which would bring with it untold joy and more than enough tears. The security of our past and the fear of the future would be the focus of our daily prayers.

Ruth's adjustment to our new circumstances was extremely smooth and seamless, while I had a much sharper learning curve. The idea of being a father was marvelous; the practical applications were somewhat less glamorous. The changing of dirty diapers, having food spit back in my face, and being up half the night with someone who couldn't tell you that they had an ear infection, took some of the shine off the nameplate "Dad."

During the early years of any marriage, there are many situations where you have the opportunity to not only learn a great deal about each other, but also to learn from each other.

An example of one of Ruth's early "teaching moments" came in the middle of one particular night when our son, David, was only a few months old. We had quickly become converted to the wonderful advantages afforded by the use of a pacifier. However, on this particular evening, David had become convinced that it was far more fun to continually spit it out than to enjoy its intended use. At some point I sat up in bed and gave the "binky," as we affectionately had come to call it, a great deal of unbridled propulsion. The sound that it made as it careened off the opposite wall of the bedroom let us all know that it had made the journey in slightly under the speed of sound. More embarrassed than mad, I got out of bed and proceeded down the stairs to regain my composure, along with some blood in my arm. With two or three steps to go, I stopped short of the living room and slowly sat down. With my hands clasped tightly together, elbows on my thighs, and head hanging down, I could hear the bedroom door close at the top of the stairs. The lights from outside showed through the windows enough so that you could make out the forms of objects within the rooms below. I heard Ruth's soft footsteps slowly coming down the stairs behind me. She sat on the stair just above the one I was on and placed her left arm around my back while resting her head on my right shoulder. Several moments passed in silence as many things were going through our minds. Finally, Ruth broke the hush with a soft and quiet voice. The words she would speak would manifest the depth of her understanding and demonstrate the strength of her character. "Don't you see that these experiences we have are a test to see what kind of parents we will be? Please don't ever do anything that might deny us the opportunity of having more children. Just say a short prayer, gather yourself back up, and come to bed. David is sound asleep. Oh, by the way, I love you."

The lesson had been taught with tenderness by someone who would teach me many more. If I could asked the angels above whom she had just referred to, if this beautiful woman, my eternal companion, was my greatest gift in life, I know I would have heard a resounding "YES."

THREE

An Unmarked Path

In my early adulthood, there was a time called "someday." It was a season in the future when I would have a career instead of a job, when my bills would be called long-term obligations, and my life would be centered around a wife and a family rather than around myself and my friends. With no regrets, I gladly conceded that "someday" was now.

In the short time that Ruth and I had been together, I had made greater strides towards my career than in all the years prior. Then, on a late summer morning in 1978, as I stood shaving in the upstairs bathroom, I heard the phone ring. Knowing that Ruth was in the bedroom, I stood still, holding my breath, so as to hear her response. "Yes, he is. Just a minute please and I'll get him." After all the years of preparation, and after all the recent interviews and tests, could this be the call we had been waiting for? I had barely turned around before she got to the doorway. With a voice full of breathless anticipation, she said, "It's Western Airlines personnel department, and they want to talk to you." Ruth and I were staring at each other intently as I picked up the phone and placed it to my ear. With each individual "yes," my voice grew progressively louder and her eyes opened wider. A quick "Thank you and good bye" was followed by a long embrace and a dozen more "yeses."

Finally, we had faith in the future with a secure career. Finally, we had hope that someday we would have that long-term obligation in the form of our own home. And at last, we had health insurance for ourselves, our little boy, and our baby girl who would arrive next year. We would need all three.

No other event in a married couple's life can compare to the glorious moment when their child makes its debut into this world. There have been months of anticipation, tempered only by moments of apprehension. The proud father often feels that this is an expression of his masculinity, while in a more dignified way, the mother reveres the honor of fulfilling her role as a woman.

The air was charged with like emotion the afternoon of November 2nd, 1979, when Shellie Lorraine Eyre drew her first breath. Following a normal pregnancy and an uneventful delivery, we beheld with wonder the beautiful child I cradled in my arms. Conceived in love, and nurtured with care, she had now filled our hearts and minds with an abundance of hope for her future. Within twenty-four hours, those fanciful dreams would succumb to the nightmare of reality.

Shellie was born in the mid-afternoon, and both Ruth and I were thankful for the few hours we could spend quietly together following the birth. With our newborn child safely in the nursery, we made the most of this interval by reminiscing on the events of the past few months and acknowledging the resplendent miracle of the present and future. Our lives and family seemed so complete. Many of those elements that comprised my concept of "someday" were now in place. I had a wonderful career, the wife and marriage of my dreams, a healthy little boy, and a beautiful baby girl. After receiving so many wonderful blessings, there was no reason to think that they would not continue.

Later on that evening, after Ruth had inquired several times, they finally brought Shellie into our room. It was then that I witnessed one of the many poignant experiences that a man will never be able to know or appreciate. It is that special moment when a woman is able to nurse her newborn child for the first time. It seems to mark the end of one stage of life and the commencement of another phase of lifelong nurturing. For the moment, I was only a spectator. However, it soon became evident that we would be denied this privilege for the time being. Ruth became equally disappointed and concerned that Shellie had failed to nurse. I tried to mitigate any anxiety by rationalizing how much Shellie had been through in the last few hours and how tired she must be. I attempted to reassure Ruth that Shellie would surely let us know when she was hungry, but until then, it was probably best for all of us to get some rest.

The following morning, I returned to the hospital as early as possible. Ruth was awake, and even the radiant glow on her face couldn't disguise her uneasiness with the fact that they had not yet brought Shellie in to her for a morning feeding.

Just as she finished voicing her concerns, the nurse entered the room, and with one cheerful "And how is everyone doing today?", erased the rayless mood and replaced it with the light of our lives. I stretched forth my hands to receive the tiny bundle, and with a rather condescending smile, the nurse passed by me and laid the child next to her mother with loving care. There was a sisterhood here that told me, without saying a word, that a certain priority existed and that I should wait my turn.

Finally, my time did come, and as I held this tiny infant, I was struck by how small and fragile she appeared. At barely half the weight of our firstborn son, I was able to cradle her head, shoulders, and back in one hand while supporting her legs and bottom in the other. I was amazed at how still she remained, and as I gazed into her face, I was overcome by the marvelous look of peaceful tranquility that seemed to penetrate my vision and go directly to my heart. How could a child this young know to look at someone else directly in their eyes? Her head turned slowly from side to side, but the focus of her attention never changed. After holding her for some time, I slowly pulled the blanket down to expose more of Shellie's upper body. For the first time, I noticed what appeared to be extra skin on the back of her neck that stretched out toward her shoulders. I asked Ruth if this appeared unusual, and she was somewhat offended that I could find anything wrong with this perfectly gorgeous child. Her main concern was directed at the fact that Shellie was not taking nourishment and asked if I would go to the desk and see when Dr. Steinmetz would be making his morning rounds. Before I could position myself to hand our child back to her, the doctor opened the door. He was a handsome man, in his early forties, with a pleasant smile and an affable personality.

As he entered the room, we could sense a change in his normal demeanor. Though his greeting was cordial, the look on his face betrayed his concern. Without even looking at Shellie, he inquired if everything was all right. After we had voiced our observations, he failed to reply for a moment as if contemplating several options. His response was short, clinical, and to the point. "With regards to the skin on the neck, that could be what we refer to as subcutaneous tissue which may be associated with Turner's syndrome. Now, Turner's syndrome is a chromosome disorder that only occurs in girls. It may or may not be affiliated with the inability of your daughter to nurse, but we do need to do a complete chromosome workup on Shellie as soon as possible. However, for right now, we need to determine why she is not eating and why she has not been able to pass any fluid. It will be necessary to take some X-rays of the digestive tract and see if there is anything out of the ordinary. I've scheduled those to be done this morning and we will know a great deal more once we can view the pictures."

The magic in the air was gone. It had been replaced with the first realization that something could be wrong. Seriously wrong.

Even though the doctor tried to place the primary importance on the fact that Shellie wasn't eating properly and that an X-ray needed to be taken, both Ruth and I sensed that this condition could be corrected. It was the idea of a chromosome disorder that begged for more explanation. Ruth had already asked the question before I could formulate what I wanted to say. The mood in the room had changed to reflect the serious nature of her inquiry: "Shellie looks so beautiful, so perfect. I know of the concerns that Ted has expressed, but I can see no evidence of a chromosome problem. What makes you feel that way? What are you seeing that I don't?" Dr. Steinmetz's response was tempered with kind uncertainty.

"The kind of digestive problem we may have here is consistent with children that have a genetic disorder. We have also noticed a lack of normal muscle tone and some features suggesting that your child may be mongoloid.(1) If so, I feel there is a chance she is a mosaic. None of this can be confirmed until we do some further tests. However, I can't overstress the necessity for the X-rays and the determination of her digestive problems. We need to exercise caution here, and take one step at a time."

Dr. Steinmetz must have felt he had given us enough information to reflect on for the time being and that he was not one to become embroiled in the "what if" game until more complete answers were known.

He politely excused himself and the room was filled with an eerie silence for a few moments while we each tried to collect our thoughts. The overpowering word "mongoloid" kept repeating itself over and over in my mind. Just moments ago, I had felt part of a happy and vibrant family. Now, if only for a few seconds, I felt the bewilderment of being alone and isolated.

Ruth immediately expressed her concern about how I was feeling, and I was just as anxious to reassure her and relieve as much apprehension as possible. For the next hour, we went over the events of the pregnancy, the ease of the delivery, and how beautiful a child Shellie was. There was no thought of anger and no place for blame. This was a time for comfort and encouragement. We then called our families to make them aware of the situation. As in any difficult circumstance, we found there is no substitute for the support of the family. We would be amazed at how many family members would answer the call.

The results of the X-rays were conclusive enough to show that there was an intestinal blockage, but inconclusive as to the extent or cause. Further tests would need to be done, but immediate surgery was an absolute necessity. Dr. Steinmetz assured us that the best facility for pediatric care of this type was across the bay at Stanford Hospital in Palo Alto. He would make the arrangements for the surgical team, transportation, and also for a geneticist to determine if Shellie had Down's syndrome.(2) That had quickly become the phrase of choice; the word "mongoloid" was regarded as far too harsh and dissonant.

A team of doctors and nurses arrived from Stanford early the next morning. What we had looked forward to as being a day that Ruth would come home with a healthy baby girl, had now been transformed into one filled with emotions of fear and anxiety. As we followed the ambulance through the city streets and across the bridge, we had to concede the fact that it was a beautiful day. The cloudless sky and cool temperature was a welcome change from the intensity of the hospital room. The relief was short lived as we rushed into the pediatric care unit in an attempt to catch up with the entourage surrounding our infant daughter.

It was quickly determined by radiological examination that there was a duodenal atresia (an intestinal obstruction) just below Shellie's stomach. Of the two possible scenarios, this was the easiest to correct surgically. However, due to Shellie's size and weakened condition, the operation was still considered extremely hazardous. Ruth's entire family was at the hospital and I sensed a continuous flow of prayers being offered up on Shellie's behalf. The support of a family in a time of crisis is something that cannot be measured, only appreciated.

Now, at three days old, instead of being in the hands of a loving parent who was contemplating her future, Shellie was in the hands of a skilled surgeon, fighting to save her life. Just a short distance away, Ruth and I sat in a private waiting room, surrounded by family, yet alone in our private thoughts. Nearly an hour had passed, the silence being broken, only occasionally, with words of comfort and reassurance. However, I felt a sudden desire to be alone. I excused myself to walk down the hall for a drink of water. I had mistakenly thought that a change of scene would temporarily relieve my anxiety. What I saw in the hall tended to unnerve me even more. People were going about, engaged in their daily routine and seemingly unaware of the intensity that consumed me. Near the end of the hall, an elevator opened up and a couple emerged, laughing at some humorous story that continued until they entered a room just a few yards away. I questioned how anyone could be laughing, reading, or watching television. The world had not stopped, only mine had, and the realization of that was far from comforting. As I returned to the room, I wondered how long it would be before our world would return to normal, or more importantly, if it ever would.

Dr. Hartman entered the room a short time later, and the modest smile on his face conveyed the eagerly awaited message before he could form the words. The surgery had gone well and Shellie was resting comfortably in the recovery room. One bridge had been crossed, but the rest of the path remained unmarked.

FOUR

Intensive Care & Understanding

"May the Lord grant me the strength to change the things I can, the courage to accept the things I cannot, and the wisdom to know the difference."

No other statement could better epitomize my progression through the various emotional phases I would encounter during the next year. As a result of the teachings of my parents, I had always come to depend on the gift of prayer to help me through difficult situations. Never before had I ever employed this lesson with such intensity.

On the second day following Shellie's operation, various doctors who had been involved in the case came by to check on her condition. It was obvious that they were concerned with our well being also, with one possible exception. Dr. Middleton(3) introduced himself as the head of the genetic department within the pediatric care unit. Ruth and I had anticipated this meeting with mixed emotions. Our concerns were well warranted. He proved to have the compassion and tactfulness of a sledgehammer.

"I'm glad to see that your daughter is recovering well from the operation. Dr. Steinmetz has asked me to consult on the case. I have concluded my primary observation and have scheduled some tests to be done, but it is obvious to me that your daughter has Down's syndrome. We should have the results of a karyotype in seven or eight days to confirm my findings, after which you should contact my office to schedule a time for genetic counseling." We were not only shocked with what he had said, but equally as much with how he had said it.

Ruth responded quickly and with as much directness. "Dr. Steinmetz has assured us that he feels that Shellie does not have Down's syndrome and that many of the symptoms are not present. With the exception of what she has just been through, Shellie appears to be like every other newborn baby. We have a lot to deal with over the next seven or eight days regarding her recovery. During that period of time we will be relying on Dr. Steinmetz's opinions."

For a moment I felt like a bystander watching two equally matched opponents sparring. He had hit a cord in Ruth, resulting in a self-assurance and conviction in her that I had not previously seen. As she stared into his face, there was no doubt who would blink first. Dr. Middleton was ill prepared for this battle, dressed only in the armor of education. Regardless of the results of the test, even he could sense he was no match for a mother defending her child's dignity.

The intensive care unit was located in the center of the third floor of the pediatric care facility. There were no outside windows that would allow a temporary escape to the exterior world. With no evidence of it being day or night, all attention seemed to focus on the six small infants, each encompassed in the controlled environment that their incubators provided. On occasion, I would find myself alone in the room and grateful for the opportunity I had to acquaint myself with its precious occupants. Some were born with serious birth defects and some were extremely premature, but each of them was clinging onto life with quiet nobility. Though a medical chart may describe in exacting detail their short physiological history, I knew that each contained a story very much like ours, a story filled with the concerns of talented doctors and loving nurses and with the hopes and prayers of parents and families. An ever-unfolding drama, containing more questions than answers, more pain than joy, and often more fear than faith.

Of all these children, Shellie appeared to us to be in the least serious condition. However, because her veins were so small or had collapsed, her I.V. had to be inserted in her head and was taped to a styrofoam cup. A rubber surgical tube that led into her stomach protruded out of the skin approximately a half-inch. This was along the incision that extended from one side of her abdomen to the other. Several electrodes extended from her small chest to a telemetry unit which recorded her heartbeat and pulse rate. With Shellie sleeping a majority of the day, there were countless hours spent watching the thin green line on the monitor as it would quietly spike upwards, return to its original line, then move to the right in continuous repetition. As I stared at the number that registered the heart beats per minute, I became fascinated at why they would suddenly increase, even though Shellie appeared to be resting peacefully. Could she be dreaming, and if so, what could she possibly be dreaming about with such limited experience on earth? I began to wonder if the reason babies can't talk is because they remember too much about heaven.

During the next several days, Ruth and I were together at the hospital throughout the day and evening. We would arrive early in the morning and put on the protective gowns which the nurses provided for us. Then we would enter the special care unit and quietly draw near to Shellie, not wanting to disturb the silence and tranquility that existed in harmony with medical technology. As I stared through the plexiglass top of the incubator, I was once again overcome by the peaceful nature of our little daughter. All too often I had been consumed with my own feelings, but now I tried to imagine what Shellie was going through. In just a few short days, she had transitioned from being in the womb, to experiencing birth, seeing her parents, going through life-threatening surgery, and now being enclosed in the claustrophobic confines of an incubator. I could only hope that she didn't think this was normal or that this would portend of things to come.

How much we looked forward to those times during the day when we could displace that barrier between us and hold her in our arms. Though verbal communication of our feelings may have been impossible at this point, I knew we could convey to her our feelings of love with the touch of our hand, the tone of our voice, and the tender way we rocked her in our arms. I seemed to sense then, how important those nonverbal expressions of love would be to her throughout her lifetime. Even now, it helped to think of times to come, to look beyond the tragedy of the moment and imagine a happy time in the future when the fears and pains of today would be but a distant memory. As all consuming as this had become, we needed to get our lives in focus again. Other priorities existed, such as our marriage, my work, and our little boy at home.

Other members of the family were caring for David, and even though he was occupied by the singular experiences of each day, he must have sensed that something was wrong. It may have been perceived by some that the reason Ruth had taped David's baby picture on the front of Shellie's incubator was to indicate that, during all the hours we spent with her, we were also thinking of him. In reality, it was a disguised attempt to call attention to the fact that Shellie looked just like our normal, healthy little boy at home. Whether this had more therapeutic effect on us than anyone else was of little consequence.

On the morning of the fifth day following Shellie's operation, I had to leave on a three-day trip. It was my first time back at work since she had been born, and in some ways, I thought the break would do me some good. What I didn't realize was that, no matter where I was or what I was doing, my thoughts constantly remained with Shellie and Ruth. Never before had I experienced a time in my life when I felt that I was in continuous prayer. Never before had I felt that I needed to be.

Those that I worked with must have perceived something was wrong. With the knowledge that I had just had a baby girl and my total lack of conversation about her, my silence must have spoken many words. Throughout the day, I would go about my work in a perfunctory manner, performing those functions required for each flight. However, during the many long hours of staring at the instrument panel, my mind would involuntarily return to a small room at Stanford Hospital.

On my first layover, I could hardly wait to get to the solitude of my hotel room. Once there, I was surprised to find that I was exhausted from thinking and praying about Shellie, and all my thoughts were focused on Ruth. How I loved her and how much I missed being with her. I was so thankful for her strength and so uplifted by her courage. She was the only person I could talk to, the only one that could truly understand my feelings. We were going through this together, a joint venture that would expose our deepest emotions and solidify the foundation of our relationship. During that evening, I came to the reassuring knowledge that, whenever life handed me things too difficult to carry alone, I had been given a companion who would willingly take half the load.

The following day consisted of three different flight segments, beginning in the mid afternoon. The late report time afforded me the opportunity to sleep in that morning and wake up without the assistance of an alarm clock. While lying in bed, I found it curious that I couldn't remember dreaming about what had dominated my thoughts before falling asleep. I felt no retention of any dream, only the heaviness of a hard and long awaited night's rest. I was grateful for the privacy and isolation that the hotel room provided. However, any desire I had for quiet seclusion was swept away as I opened the blinds to a spectacular, clear morning in Vancouver, British Columbia. The sparkling vista removed any desire for reclusiveness and replaced it with an urgency to fill my lungs with the cool morning air. I showered and dressed as if late for an appointment and was two or three steps down the hall before I heard the door close behind me. It was a straight line from the elevator and across the lobby to the large revolving door. As I stepped out on the sidewalk, I paused to take the anticipated deep breath. The cold air seemed to clear my head more than to satisfy my lungs. I had taken two long breaths before I opened my eyes with the realization that I was smiling. Smiling. How long had it been since I had last smiled? By merely lifting the corners of my mouth, I felt I had raised a weight off my shoulders.

Few people were on the streets and most of the stores were still closed on this weekend morning as I leisurely walked, without direction, loitering only occasionally to observe a window display. My focus would change from the sweater or coat to my reflection in the glass, and I discovered how a barely noticeable grin had more of an effect on the attitude of my heart than it did on the expression of my face. Maybe it was the change of my environment that resulted in the alteration of my attitude, but without explanation, I could sense the relief from the rest of the crew as we drove to the airport and engaged in unimportant conversation. My thoughts and prayers were still with Shellie, but the oppressive intensity had noticeably diminished.

Our flight to Portland was uneventful and I eagerly awaited the next leg to San Francisco where I would have plenty of time to call home. The schedule indicated there would be an airplane change for us before continuing on to Los Angeles for the night.

Our approach to the city brought us along the coast and on the outside of the Golden Gate Bridge. The clear, beautiful night made for a sparkling display of lights far past San Jose and extending well beyond all the cities of the East Bay. My eyes followed the line of headlights that made up the Bay Shore Freeway, and from the intersection with the San Mateo Bridge, I tried to imagine the location of the Stanford Hospital. However, the attention necessary for the approach made this only a temporary diversion.

After the passengers had deplaned, the rest of the crew continued downstairs to the lounge in order to get away from the noisy confusion of the terminal. I excused myself to make a phone call, but actually walked across the concourse to the gate from which our flight would depart. With well over an hour before its expected arrival, there was no one at the ticket counter and only a few people in the waiting area. I made my way to the door above which was a large sign indicating Gate 56. After entering the security code, I continued down the dark and deserted jetway. Even without an airplane filling the large opening where I placed my bags, there was a sense of quietness in a place usually filled with the sounds of jet engines. The entire ramp area was deserted as I gazed over the expansion of concrete that extended to distant cargo facilities across the field. It felt good to be back in such a familiar environment, yet quickly, this image drifted back to the foreign surroundings of a hospital just a few miles away.

I was impressed to take advantage of this solitude and offer a short prayer before returning to the terminal to call Ruth. What transpired in the following few minutes was something I had never experienced before in my life. As I closed my eyes and slightly lowered my head, a single word seemed to just roll off my lips. "Father." My eyes shot open. I was stunned at what I had said.

Never before had I begun a prayer in such an informal way. I was at first alarmed or scared that I had been so irreverent. I had always begun a prayer with a more formal "My Father in Heaven," and I was now shocked at how natural and intimate this petition felt. It brought with it the sensation of a young boy asking his dad for help. After analyzing my thoughts for a short time, I once again closed my eyes, and in a much quieter way, repeated the single word, then paused for a feeling of acceptance. I continued with a prayer that felt more like a conversation than the one-way communication I was used to. I had not completed my earnest appeal before, once again, I was stopped in mid-sentence. There was a voice that spoke in my heart, as clear as any I had ever heard with my ear, that said, "Shellie will be all right." It seemed to repeat itself several times, as if for confirmation. Before I gave any thought to finishing the prayer, I ran up the jetway and bolted through the door.

I failed to notice if my abrupt entrance surprised anyone. I raced towards the closest phone. In my excitement, I found I had to consciously focus on remembering my phone number. When Ruth answered, I barely gave her a chance to speak before relating my experience of just a few minutes ago. I tried to reassure her that the message, impression, or what ever it was, was meant for us. That with only one or two days left before the results of the genetic tests, we could stop worrying. I repeated the words over and over: "Shellie will be all right, Shellie will be all right."

As we concluded our conversation, I couldn't wait for an end to this trip. I visualized the moment when I could visit our daughter and look at her, for the first time, with a renewed hope for things to come.

Upon returning the following day, I drove directly from the airport to the hospital parking lot. I was anxious not only to see Shellie and Ruth, but eager to find out if the test results had been reported. As I approached the room and looked through the glass before opening the door, I could see Ruth sitting alone next to Shellie. Though it had been difficult being away for three days, I felt somewhat renewed. Ruth had enjoyed no such break, and even though there still existed a sublime nature around her, the constant drain on emotions had to have been exhausting. I slowly opened the door and her eyes turned away from the magazine to meet mine. An affable smile formed on her face as we began to communicate without speaking a word. As I perceived her saying with her eyes, "Hello, sweetheart. It's good to see you," I answered her back by raising my eyebrows and tilting my head. She comprehended the silent question, and slowly closed her eyes and shook her head from side to side. Not wanting to break the quiet moment, Ruth gave to me the time to gaze at our daughter and collect my thoughts. Shellie was resting so calmly and there was a noticeable improvement in the color of her skin. Without disturbing her or the serenity of the room, I slowly turned back to Ruth and whispered, "Let's go home and have dinner with David." With a nearly unperceivable nod, Ruth affirmed the idea and we quietly exited the room.

The stillness continued until we reached the elevator when, in a hushed voice, Ruth said, "The test results might be in this evening." The ride home contained little conversation and a lot of quiet contemplation.

The evening with David provided a welcome diversion, yet each time the phone would ring, it would convert the noise and activity to motionless silence. Both of us would hold our breath until the one answering the phone shook their head in the negative, and the conventional routine would slowly return. About eight o'clock that evening, David was upstairs playing and Ruth was picking up toys in the front room. I had decided to go to the store as we both thought it beyond the time that we would hear from the hospital. Just as I was starting the car, the phone rang in the kitchen. With the fingers of her left hand pressed gently across her mouth and her eyes closed, Ruth breathlessly voiced, "Hello."

She recognized the voice instantly. "Ruth, this is Dr. Shocket and I have the result of the..."

"Stop, wait," she interrupted, "I've got to get Ted before he leaves."

I was just backing out of the driveway when Ruth came rushing out of the house and placed both hands on the passenger window. "He's on the phone. Dr. Shocket is on the phone."

Not returning the car up the driveway, but placing it in park and grabbing the keys, I ran into the house with Ruth just behind me. Her eyes were riveted on my face for the first sign or indication of the news. Following my initial "Yes" Dr. Shocket's voice was very professional yet fused with compassion.

"Mr. Eyre, we have the results from the karyotype and they verify that your daughter has Down's syndrome. She is a trisomy 21 which is by far the most common chromosome disorder. When you come into the hospital tomorrow, we would be glad to arrange some genetic counseling at your convenience."

The look of shock on my face transmitted the message to Ruth as quickly as if she had heard the words herself. Before I could say "Thank you and good-bye," all the welled-up emotions of nearly two weeks burst out of her as she covered her face with both hands and ran from the kitchen.

Through a torrent of tears she kept repeating, "No, no. This can't be. It just can't be." Seeing David motionless on the landing half way down the stairs, she rushed to him and fell to her knees as she pressed him close to her chest. Like a dazed little man, he stood there trying to comprehend the confusing atmosphere. I slowly walked out of the kitchen in an emotionless state of shock and disbelief. Too stunned to cry, I made my way to the first stair just above where Ruth still clung to David. As I sat down behind her, no words of comfort would come to mind, no gesture of empathy seemed to be adequate. As I stared straight forward in absolute silence, Ruth slowly turned to me, and catching her breath, said, "Where is the answer to our prayers now?" The words traversed my heart and went to my very soul. She had described my only prevailing thought. This was not the question of a faithless woman, but the petition of an anguished mother.

David remained silently still, not understanding the scene, but comprehending the comfort he provided for his mother. He was her anchor in this emotional storm. In a myriad of confusing thoughts, I felt incapable of forming an appropriate or consoling response. There was no script to go by, no correct or well-suited thing to do or say. Each of us would cope with this trial in an individual way. I chose the solitude of our upstairs bedroom. Behind closed doors, I questioned if I should pray or what I should pray about, and more importantly, if there really existed someone to pray to. The very foundation of my beliefs had suffered a devastating blow. What did it mean, "Shellie will be all right?" Had I said that to myself? Had I been communing all these years with no one but myself? What was left of me without my beliefs?

I had envisioned my role as the spiritual head of the house. Ruth had always been the spiritual heart of our family. I knew that the sooner the head could come to reason, the quicker the heart would begin to mend.

My thoughts drifted to examples of others and how they had endured set backs or losses much greater than mine. I had admired stories of those who had demonstrated great strength and character in the face of adversity. I began to realize that the only thing I had lost was an appropriate perspective. How could this one disappointment overshadow all that we had? In just a few quiet moments, the healing had begun.

FIVE

The Learning Curve

If there was a positive side to learning the results of the genetic test, it was that the anxiety and uncertainty was over. We now knew what we were facing and that we were going to work through this together.

Even though each of us would deal with the shock, denial, and grief in our own personal way, we had chosen to keep those thoughts private and to encourage the other with more constructive reasoning.

Throughout our drive to Palo Alto the following morning, it was generally agreed that the more positive attitude we had, the more rapid our adjustment would be. We knew this acclimation would not only benefit us, but David, our family and most importantly, Shellie. We were smart enough to know we had a difficult journey ahead, but not wise enough to know the wonderful places it would take us.

As we arrived at the special care unit, we could sense a cautious demeanor by the nurses we had come to know so well. Each of them seemed hesitant and uncertain as to how we had taken the news. Our relaxed tenor seemed to quickly disarm their collective fears.

It was difficult to tell if the perceived improvement in Shellie's condition was due to her determined recovery or from our different perspective. Over the last twenty-four hours, it was unclear who had healed the most. Before leaving the hospital that evening, we had made an appointment for the following morning for genetic counseling. It could only be hoped that our second encounter with Dr. Middleton would prove to be more congenial than the first.

A steady rain, combined with early morning commute traffic, provided a credible excuse for the lack of conversation en route to our nine o'clock meeting. However, more thought was being given to our inward anxiety than to the other cars and road conditions. As we pulled into the parking lot reserved for the administrative and office buildings, I passed by several stalls restricted to handicapped parking. For the first time, I felt a personal identification with the rights given to the disabled. Several comments passed through my mind, none of which were appropriate for the delicate atmosphere of the moment.

Following the directions given to us the previous day, we easily found the first floor office. Adjacent to the door was a full-length glass panel. At the top was painted the office number and in the middle were three names, each preceded with the prefix "Dr." Obviously not in alphabetical order, it could only be assumed they were arranged by seniority. Dr. Middleton was first on the list.

After the ordinary introduction, we had barely sat down before the receptionist called our name and politely stepped aside as she opened the dark, paneled door. Upon entering the office, Dr. Middleton stood up from behind his desk and invited us to be seated in the two armchairs directly in front of him. Numerous papers covered his desk and on each end were unorganized stacks of books. Behind him was an oak credenza containing more books and papers, but obviously void of any pictures of friends or family. The "I love me" wall above the credenza contained a myriad of framed certificates, indicating the necessity of a multitude of different licenses, or that he had mounted every document and diploma since grade school. I was sure, if I looked hard enough, I would be able to find one thanking him for being a member of the National Geographic Society.

Each of us tried to find a comfortable position in our respective chairs as Dr. Middleton removed the reading glass snagged on the end of his nose. I had hoped that his cordial greeting was based on sincerity rather than on an attempt to patronize someone whom he had failed to intimidate the week before. As he leaned back in his chair and folded his arms across his chest, we knew that the presentation was about to begin.

"Having received the results of the tests, I assume you have many questions. Have you had an opportunity to read any information on Down's syndrome, for instance, what causes it, and the long term outlook for you and your child?" My response was a reluctant "no."

Ruth elaborated a bit more. "It's only been a little over a day since we received the news from Dr. Shocket. Prior to that, we were hoping it wouldn't be necessary."

"Well, let me begin by explaining what we know about Down's syndrome, both genetically and historically. Prior to the mid 1800's, little if anything was known about this. Then, a British physician by the name of Langdon Down described a condition he called mongolism. If I remember right, he believed that mental retardation fell into several categories based on the physical characteristics of the affected individuals. The reason it was initially called mongolism, was because the facial features of young victims seemed to resemble those of orientals. But it wasn't until about 1959 that a French pediatrician named Jerome Lejeune discovered that the condition was caused by a chromosomal abnormality. That's when these types of disorders really began to be understood. You have probably heard some of us refer to a karyotype. Maybe you remember them from your biology classes in high school or college. This is where cells are grown in a culture for about a week, then photographed and paired together, numbering from one to twenty-three in accordance with their decreasing size. Paired, is the important word here because there are only supposed to be two chromosomes in each group. However, in your daughter's case, there are three chromosomes in the number twenty-one group, and that abnormality exists in every cell in her body. Now, before we get involved in how this all happened, let me just tell you that this is the most common identifiable form of mental retardation there is. It occurs in one out of every one thousand live births. That represents about five thousand children being born with this condition each year in the United States alone. Unfortunately, there can be many associated problems with this congenital defect which we will discuss later. What we can focus on now is how this came about."

Dr. Middleton had captured my undivided attention since his opening statement. I couldn't remember moving a single time in the chair except when he said certain words which caused me to involuntarily wince each time I heard them. Words such as "abnormality," "retarded," and "defect" made me instantly close my eyes and try to draw up a mental picture of each term. Quickly, I would try to refocus on the next thing he was saying in order not to miss out on some vital information. His explanation so far had been easy to understand, but I could sense, as he took a long slow breath before continuing, that he was wondering how to restructure, in lay terms, a highly medical concept.

He then continued, "Every cell in your body has forty-six chromosomes with the exception of the cells in the ovum and sperm. They are made up of twenty-three chromosomes, and when they come together, at the moment of conception, each chromosome in the mother's egg is matched with the corresponding chromosome of the father's sperm. Now we have a cell with forty-six chromosomes, or twenty-three pairs, twenty-two of which are responsible for the various hereditary traits, and the last pair for determining the sex of the child. Simple enough, right? Well, this process, called meiosis, is far from simple. For one reason or another, in your case, either the egg or the sperm contained an extra chromosome; that is, two chromosome twenty-ones prior to conception. Therefore, when they came together, there were now three chromosomes in the number twenty-one group instead of the normal two. This extra chromosome, in the vast majority of cases, is thought to be in the egg rather than the sperm. The only explanation I might have for this is that the mother is born with all the eggs she will ever have, while the father produces new sperm about every ninety-six hours. There are other types of Down's syndrome that result from translocation, but we needn't get involved in those. However, I know Dr. Steinmetz mentioned mosaicism to you, where the error in cell division occurs after the egg has been fertilized, therefore affecting only part of the cells in the body. But that is not the case here. Any questions with the physiology of all this?"

Neither Ruth nor I answered for several seconds as the words "meiosis," "translocation," and "mosaicism" settled down in our minds. Finally, I looked over at her and answered for both of us, "No." I thought to myself, *we have some serious reading to do.* The line on the learning curve had just begun to go vertical.

With his head tilted slightly up from his concluding question, Dr. Middleton slowly began to lower his focus along with the seriousness of his voice. He looked at us as if to measure our maturity more than our understanding. We were totally unprepared with what lay ahead.

"We need to address now the decisions you will be facing in the near future. You can only reach a conclusion after understanding all the facts. They may not be pleasant, but they need to be realized. I'm sure you know that your daughter will be severely mentally and physically retarded. She will have poor muscle tone and be prone to respiratory infections and possible heart defects. These children also have a much higher rate of leukemia and, obviously, a shorter life span than normal. I understand you have a young son at home, and he and his welfare must be taken into consideration also. All too often, these siblings become the forgotten ones, as so much attention must be given to the severely disabled child. What results, then, is that you ultimately have a handicapped family. My suggestion to you is that you place this child in an institution, where it can be properly cared for, and go on with your life."

For a brief moment I felt totally disoriented by not knowing rather to react to the thoughts of my mind, or the emotions of my heart. But in the confusion of disbelief and anger, the enmity I felt towards this individual exceeded any antagonism I could have previously imagined. I could hardly envision the resentment and rage welling up in Ruth. The question was now if the large oak desk represented a sufficient barrier between him and us? The only prudent action was to leave as quickly as possible. I abruptly stood straight up and stared at him, motionless. As Ruth came to her feet and looked at me, I couldn't tell if the expression on her face was that of shock from what she had just heard or fear of what I might do next. After taking a deep breath, I held it while I released the words, "I don't think you realize, Shellie is our life!" Several long seconds passed in silence before we turned towards the door. Just before I reached for the handle, Ruth stopped and slowly turned around, and with one silent stare, removed any doubt its receiver could have had that she would ever return.

Not a word was said until we reached the car. Once inside, we constantly interrupted each other as we expressed our similar disdain and disgust of what we had just heard. Finally, we both stopped at the same time, realizing we were stepping all over what the other was saying. After several seconds of silence, I broke into a smile and said, "Well, I think we both agree on that." The ensuing laughter seemed to totally discharge the heat of the moment. Ruth slowly shook her head from side to side and looked up at the roof of the car as she concluded our thoughts, "Let's get out of here." The rain had stopped, the sun was now breaking through the clouds, and suddenly, everything seemed to be more clear.

During Shellie's prolonged stay in the hospital, we saw her continuing to improve and gaining strength each week. Throughout that time, we read as much material as we could find on Down syndrome from various bookstores and libraries. Often times the literature was quite old and representative of a cynical outlook. Many of the pictures of the children were of those who were institutionalized, and their faces seemed to reflect the depressed and gloomy atmosphere they lived in. This seemed to intensify Ruth's feelings that this would not be Shellie's fate. She was determined our little daughter would be aware of our love and respect for her and that Shellie would feel secure and protected from fear or self doubt. The insight of a loving mother had affirmed her conviction that Shellie would become what she pictured herself and the world to be. Ruth was convinced this could only come about if we had a healthy attitude about ourselves, along with an appropriate amount of personal dignity. It was amazing to me how a little bit of common sense and positive thinking was better than a lot of uncaring counseling.

We finally received the news that Shellie would be able to leave the hospital within the first week of December. We had the house all ready and looked forward to integrating her into all the family activities. In whatever way we could, we wanted to prove that we would not be a handicapped family and that our lifestyle would remain as normal as possible.

When Shellie left the hospital, she still weighed only slightly over five pounds. Even baby clothes were too big for her. So after a trip to the toy store, she came home dressed as the doll she truly was.

The uncertain adjustments when bringing a new baby home are always interesting. As a form of introduction, Shellie brought David a wonderful gift from the hospital. No one corrected him when he perceived it had come directly from heaven. He seemed to sense his new position was that of Shellie's fearless protector.

Once we were all settled in and unpacked, the opportunity finally came to feed Shellie for the first time at home. To make the transition even easier, the nurse at the hospital had premixed a formula bottle for us. Shellie still had the rubber tube sticking out from her stomach in case of any emergency. If things went as planned, it would be removed just prior to Christmas. As Ruth got in a comfortable position on the couch, I handed her the bottle. After only a few seconds of having the nipple in her mouth, Shellie's head shot back and her arms flew outward. Her face had turned blue and it was obvious she was choking. After Ruth turned her over and cleared the formula from her mouth, everyone took a few minutes to catch their breath. Following a call to the hospital, it was discovered that the formula had been mixed at double the strength. It was an abrupt reminder that, even with the best of intentions, sometimes mistakes can be made. Regardless of the age of the child, I was learning that a parent would never totally relax.

Prior to Christmas, we returned to Stanford on several occasions for follow-up appointments. Then, on December 24th, Shellie received her first present from Dr. Shocket. He simply reached down and pinched the rubber tube between his index finger and thumb. With a quick snap of his wrist the tube was out. He assured us the stomach would heal and a few small stitches were the only evidence that the tube was ever there. Christmas of 1979 would truly be a joyous time for all of us, and the new year would begin a period of continuing education that would last a lifetime.

The following is by Emily Perl Kingsley(4) and is called

"Welcome to Holland":

"I am often asked to describe the experience of raising a child with a disability--to try to help people who have not shared that unique experience to understand it, to imagine how it would feel.

It's like this...

When you're going to have a baby, it's like planning a fabulous vacation trip--to Italy. You buy a bunch of guidebooks and make your wonderful plans. The Coliseum, the Michelangelo David, the gondolas in Venice. You may learn some handy phrases in Italian. It's all very exciting.

After months of eager anticipation, the day finally arrives. You pack your bags and off you go. Several hours later, the plane lands.

The stewardess comes in and says 'Welcome to Holland.'

'Holland?' you say, 'What do you mean, Holland? I signed up for Italy. I'm supposed to be in Italy. All my life I've dreamed of going to Italy.

But there has been a change in the flight plan. They've landed in Holland and there you must stay.

The important thing is that they haven't taken you to a horrible, disgusting, filthy place, full of pestilence, famine and disease. It's just a different place.

So you must go and buy new guidebooks. And you must learn a whole new language. And you will meet a whole new group of people you would never have met.

It's just a different place. It's slower-paced than Italy, less flashy than Italy. But after you've been there for a while and you catch your breath, you look around, and you begin to notice that Holland has windmills, Holland has tulips, Holland even has Rembrandts.

But everyone you know is busy coming and going from Italy, and they're all bragging about what a wonderful time they had there. And for the rest of your life, you will say, "Yes, that's where I was supposed to go. That's what I had planned.'

The pain of that will never, ever, ever, go away, because the loss of that dream is a very significant loss.

But if you spend your life mourning the fact that you didn't get to Italy, you may never be free to enjoy the very special, the very lovely things about Holland."

Ruth and I were planning on that hypothetical trip to Italy. We had made wonderful plans and anxiously awaited the arrival of our little daughter. When we found out the flight plan had been changed, we were at first devastated to say the least. But throughout the remainder of that first year, we began to see that a different world doesn't mean an awful world or one that is even inferior to the one imagined. We had been guided to a destination populated by loving and caring people, individuals who had unselfishly dedicated their lives to others seemingly less fortunate than themselves. We would be forever influenced by their acts of compassion and kindness. Certainly we would learn from new guidebooks about such things as gross motor development or fine motor skills. But more importantly, our lives would be continually enriched by a little girl who would teach us about unfiltered love and divine nature. It is a humbling experience to progress through the various phases of shock, disbelief, denial, guilt, and grief. But, it is in the fires of trial that a person's character is forged. I had much to learn about myself, but I was beginning to understand that there were some very special, very lovely things about Holland.

SIX

An Ever Changing Landscape

The Chinese have an ancient saying, "May you not live in interesting times." The following month would usher in a new decade that was often far more interesting than many of us wanted it to be. One that was filled with events that would change the course of world history: the fall of the Soviet Union and the sweeping changes brought on by Mikhail Gorbachev; chaos in China, with over a million people demonstrating for democracy in Beijing's Central Square; and after twenty-eight years, the opening of the Berlin Wall to the West.

Within our own country, we would witness the terror of our citizens being held hostage in Iran, an attempted assassination of our President, the explosion of the space shuttle Challenger, and the senseless shooting of John Lennon.

But there would be great moments of triumph in medicine and technology. Dr. Barney Clark would receive the first artificial heart, and the spacecraft Voyager 2 would begin to unlock the secrets of the universe.

We would witness wonderful advancements for women, with Sandra Day O'Connor being nominated to the Supreme Court, Geraldine Ferraro running for Vice-President, and Sally Ride winging her way into history as the first female astronaut.

Like a microcosm of the events occurring in the world around us, our family, too, would be altered with the sadness of death and the disillusionment accompanying the unexpected. Yet, these experiences would be overshadowed by the birth of two more children and the glory of watching a family become complete.

It was a world made up of good and evil, a country filled with both triumph and tragedy, and a family maturing as miracles evolved from adversity. We live in an era where the only thing that remains constant is change.

Our country would begin 1980 with a new administration in the White House that would last for eight years. Our family began the new year with a recent arrival of a sweet spirit that would endure forever.

In so many ways, Shellie's first year was characteristic of most newborn children. It was filled with the new and amazing wonders of life. Sometimes it was dark and sometimes it was light. Often she was hungry and then she was full. Mommy and daddy seemed so much larger, but a curly haired little boy didn't seem much bigger at all. And what could explain this white furry thing, with a tail and four little legs, that sometimes would lick her on the cheek and often make the same odd sound over and over again? Even for a Stanford graduate, this was all quite confusing.

Shellie's acceptance of all these diverse and unique experiences seemed swift and complete. Each morning, instead of hearing the cry of a newborn infant, Ruth and I would awaken to the sound of Shellie babbling on and on in a conversation with herself. Only when we would peer over the sides of the crib and inquire as to with whom she was talking would she stop and break into a smile that would light up the room.

We soon learned that the term "early intervention" was very appropriately named. We were amazed at the amount and quality of specialized resources available to handicapped children. Within two months of coming home from the hospital, a caring young social worker would come by our house weekly. She would spend hours teaching Shellie, along with us, about postural-motor development and self initiated activities like rolling over and reaching for objects. Shellie was a willing and happy student, seemingly loving so much wonderful attention. However, because there is such a wide range of development in a child under one year of age, Shellie seemed so normal that we, along with many of our family and friends, wondered if there really was anything wrong. We didn't begin to feel that there was a decline in Shellie's advancement until after her first birthday. However, there had been no regression on Shellie's part, only the use of a different grading criteria by us.

She soon advanced beyond being taught at home and was actively involved in a school not far from our house. Working with a dedicated teacher like Rosia Smith and with agencies like Crippled Children made us appreciate, all the more, the many blessings we had been given.

The close proximity of all of Ruth's family continued to provide a loving support that could not have been equaled in any other way. Whether I was at home or away, they were always there to assist with Shellie or to take David to the park to play.

My job had provided the opportunity for me to travel throughout the West and visit much of my family. They, too, like Ruth's family, were always there to provide a shoulder to lean on, a listening ear, and a voice to reassure. That traveling advantage came to an abrupt end on New Year's Eve of 1981.

Due to a combination of several unrelated events, Western Airlines and much of the industry had been required to lay off many of its pilots during the last few months. My number came up on January 1st. We were initially told we would be furloughed for a six-month period. It would turn out to be ten times longer. The disappointment of losing a job that I loved so much was compounded by the fear of the loss of health insurance for my family. With David in preschool, Shellie advancing so well, and the comfort of having Ruth's family just blocks away, the idea of leaving the area seemed out of the question.

Within a short period of time and with the help of some friends, I was able to get a job with a local insulation company. Crawling under sub-floors to install insulation was a long way from flying a 727, but during this experience, I learned a great deal about myself and had the opportunity of working with some wonderful people. What I thought would be a short-term occupation nearly became a career. For five years, it would provide for my family, and within that time, there would develop a friendship that would last a lifetime.

Six months prior to being laid off at the airlines, Ruth and I had learned of a reportedly, revolutionary treatment for Down syndrome children being offered in Germany. This was referred to as live cell or sicca cell therapy. It consisted of injecting freeze-dried cells from various organs of cattle and sheep into an individual. The idea was that these cells would migrate to and revitalize the corresponding organs within the affected child.

Though we had navigated through most of the predictable phases thus far, the possibility of any cure or of even the opportunity for significant improvement of Shellie's condition was an idea too enticing to pass up. The first appointment we could get was in the spring of 1981. We had no idea at the time we made the appointment that we would no longer be working for Western Airlines, have very little financial resources, and absolutely no flight benefits.

Not wanting to cancel or reschedule this long-awaited appointment, I presented our dilemma to our chief pilot in San Francisco. Having flown with Capt. Marty Farber several times over the past year, we had become friends and I had hoped he would allow us to fly to and from the east coast on Western Airlines. From there, I would be able to buy a ticket for us to Germany and back with the money we had put away for the trip. He informed me that he would look into it and told me to return the following day. The next morning, as I entered his office, Marty handed me three round trip tickets from San Francisco to Frankfurt on an international carrier. He never explained the details of this gracious gift, but I often wondered if it was the result of a daring initiative on my part or an example of "knock and the door shall be opened."

Within two months of our return from Germany, a number of changes, once again, would alter our direction in life. Some of them were short term, and others were eternal in nature. With financial conditions worsening at Western Airlines, it became evident to all that I would be furloughed for much longer than six months. However, the thought of never being called back was something I refused to accept. This optimistic outlook was brought about, most likely, by the season of the year we were just entering.

Spring always brings with it the hope of better things to come. From the first time we notice the buds beginning to appear on the trees to when we see a newborn colt standing next to its mother, we are reminded of the resplendent rejuvenation of nature. The Creator of the seasons must have realized how badly we would need this annual renewal of faith.

Our family was definitely not exempt from the daily trials that faced each one of us, but the realization and understanding of continuous new blessings, gave me a sense of a perpetual springtime.

I had recently been offered a position within the insulation company as a salesman and estimator. For hours, I would sit behind a desk and determine the amount of insulation needed in a new building by looking at page after page of blueprints. It was exciting to learn something new and I welcomed the reprieve from crawling through attics and being covered with fiberglass. As I sat in my office one morning in early June, the secretary told me my wife was on the phone. Making a quick note as to where I was on the set of plans, I spun around in my chair and picked up the phone. The tone of Ruth's voice let me know this was not an ordinary call. "Are you sitting down?" she inquired.

"With the number of plans I have spread around in here, there isn't much room to stand," I explained. "Just tell me, is it good news or bad news?"

"Well," she replied, "it's exciting news." I was reminded, once again, of that old Chinese saying, and I wasn't sure if I really wanted to be excited.

"Okay, I know, we've inherited a lot of money."

"Nope," she quickly interrupted, "it's better than that." In silence, I waited for her to continue. She sang the next two words with the first syllable of the second word being slightly higher than the others. "I'm pregnant."

Fortunately, the first words that came to my mind were not those that came to my mouth. "Oh, that's wonderful," I said. "How and when did you find this out?" The question was asked with more of intent to give me time to think than it was to divulge an answer. All I could see were dollar signs and a two-bedroom apartment with three young children. This gave a different meaning to the saying "a close family."

Shaking this image from my mind, I inquired, "Are you... scared about this?" Ruth's spirit was far too high to let an ill-timed question bring her down.

"Nope," she replied, "but I hope you get a bonus this month, because we're going to need it for the phone bill." This month! I was thinking far beyond the phone bill.

Once the euphoria of the moment subsided, we both agreed that we would heed only one piece of advice we had received from Dr. Middleton. We would schedule both an ultrasound (sonogram) to see if everything appeared all right and an amniocentesis to determine if there were any genetic abnormalities. However, this was not in order to allow us to take any measures toward terminating the pregnancy. We both shared steadfast convictions in that regard. It was simply to relieve any anxiety and acknowledge that forewarned was forearmed.

On the day of the tests, I was required to be at work. Ruth's mother drove her up to the hospital in Oakland. Throughout the thirty-minute drive, their conversation was one of encouraging anticipation circumscribed with apprehension. After the customary dialogue between doctor and patient and the clear jelly had been spread on Ruth's stomach, there, for the first time in her life, a grandmother stared in awe and wonder at the sight of her unborn grandchild. The grip of their hands grew tighter and tighter as the tears of joy rolled down their cheeks. "I can't tell for sure," the doctor interrupted, "but she appears to be a little girl."

With a trembling voice, Ruth responded, "I think I can tell, because I can even see her dimples." Three noble generations of women were caught in a quiet and magical moment in time.

A week later, while we were house sitting for Ruth's brother and sister-in-law, the call came from the doctor's office. Knowing the circumstances surrounding this case, the nurse chose not to add to the trepidation and quickly announced that the tests indicated that our child was perfectly healthy. Asking if we wanted to know the sex, Ruth responded in the affirmative, since we had previously discussed this option. "Well, I can't guarantee the dimples", the nurse said, "but I can guarantee that it's a little girl." Once again our prayers had been answered, our dreams had been fulfilled, and we would all sleep more soundly tonight.

In early August of 1981, at the age of twenty-one months, Shellie took her first steps. After so much hard work, the joy of seeing her walk between the two of us made for an emotional moment we will not forget. She had literally begun a very long path toward her independence.

Emotions of a different kind came only a few days later as my father surrendered to a long battle with cancer, just two days prior to my thirty-fifth birthday. I can honestly say that, throughout my life, no one had a greater impact on me than my dad. There was no need for me to look outside the walls of my own home to find the perfect role model. He was my champion and my friend. He had been able to know and love two of our children in this life, but would come to know and love two others in a vastly different realm. The day will come when we will be together again.

The landscape of life continued to change for us as we were asked by my company to relocate to Seattle. The opportunities provided for us there were only exceeded by the challenges. My time was consumed with trying to put a new business together. Ruth had the more daunting task of putting a new home together. Finding a nice house and good schools proved far easier than finding the right doctor. Her first appointment with Dr. Morris(5) would be her last. Once he found out she had a Down syndrome child at home, he took the offensive or, at least, became offensive. He informed Ruth that she had no business having another child and that she should seriously look into putting Shellie into an institution as soon as possible. How could anyone have so much education and continue to be so stupid? The characters were different, but we had seen this act before. Through the persistence of a new friend, we were able to get into the practice of Drs. Heller and Hodges. Our experience with Dr. Hodges proved to be one of mutual trust and respect. It culminated on December 11, 1981, as he allowed me to assist in the birth of the most beautiful baby girl I had ever seen. I always thought most babies looked like Mr. McGoo before they have a chance to "thaw out," but Amanda Jane Eyre had a radiance about her from the moment she took her first breath. Shellie had a sister. Soon they would be playmates. Eventually, they would become best friends.

In April of 1982, I was given an opportunity to return to California as the vice president of Williams Insulation. We had met some wonderful people in Washington, but the chance to return home and be with the family again was an answer to our prayers.

We found a home just several blocks from Ruth's parents and settled into enjoying the summer months filled with backyard barbecues, Kool-Aid stands, and warm, relaxing evenings. David was now riding a bike, Shellie was walking all over the house, and no crib or playpen was ever invented that Amanda couldn't crawl out of. Life was on track, but a major derailment lay just moments ahead.

June 26, 1982. I was at work, David was outside playing, and Amanda was temporarily in her crib. Ruth turned on the television and set Shellie on the couch before going into the kitchen. Moments later, after sensing something was wrong, she returned to the front room where she found Shellie lying on the carpet. As Ruth gently picked her up, there was something strange in the way Shellie responded. After sitting her back on the couch, Ruth knelt down in front of her, noticing a lack of normal expression on her face. The fact that Shellie made no attempt to return to the habit of sucking her left thumb made Ruth aware of an odd limpness on that side of her body. Slowly, Ruth reached up with her hand and softly pushed on Shellie's right shoulder. Making no attempt at protective extension, Shellie fell to the left like a little rag doll.

Ruth ran to the phone. The first call was to her sister-in-law to inquire if she could come over and watch the kids, and the second call was to me at work. The anxiousness in her voice made it evident that there was no time for a lengthy explanation. Mary arrived at our house as I was leaving the office, but due to the distance involved, Ruth arrived at the hospital well before I did. Shellie was with the doctors and Ruth was too afraid to voice her fears. The only appropriate action was to hold her in my arms and quietly wait. Within a short time, a young emergency room doctor came into the small waiting area and sat down across from us. Slowly looking up from the floor and into our eyes, he said,

"It appears that your daughter has had a stroke. We are getting no response to any stimulation of the entire left side of her body. There is no way of telling right now the extent or duration of the paralysis. We will know a great deal more after we perform a CAT-scan. The next forty-eight to seventy-two hours will be critical in our evaluation of her condition." No words were adequate to describe our feelings. Ruth buried her face in her hands and I simply closed my eyes and shook my head from side to side.

After all that hard work, Shellie had only been able to enjoy the thrill of walking on those strong little legs for ten short months. The arm that would reach out for me each day as I came home from work now lay lifeless against her side. The smile that could lighten up an entire room and bring joy to your heart had been reduced to an involuntary frown. As optimistic as I had always tried to be, it was difficult to imagine that the sun could be shining on the other side of this dark cloud. In a private moment, while waiting outside the radiology room, a previously forbidden phrase escaped my lips: "I give up." That desperate thought was replaced with guilt, as moments later I looked into Shellie's face and knew that she never would.

Later, as Ruth and I watched the technicians make the preparations for the CAT-scan, I was forced to interrupt. "What are you doing?" I demanded.

"We have to strap your daughter down to the table to ensure that she won't move during the procedure."

In a tone that conveyed corrective instruction I firmly said, "You don't have to strap her down! All you need to do is tell her not to move and she won't." With disregard for politeness, I pushed my way in between them and leaned over our motionless and frightened little girl. "Sweetheart, they're going to put you through this machine and take a picture of your head. There is nothing to be afraid of and I promise it won't hurt you, but you have to stay very still. You'll be all right and it will only take a couple of minutes. Just don't move, okay?" I could tell she understood the point of my conversation by the look of trust in her eyes. The CAT-scan was performed without complications.

With Shellie resting comfortably in her room, we sought further explanation from her doctors on what had caused the stroke.

Not until the following day did we learn that what was thought to be a cured ear infection had been misdiagnosed and the deep inflammation in her neck had most likely interrupted the adequate blood flow to her brain. Somehow, the knowledge of that did little to ease the pain.

The following day, Ruth came down with bronchitis. The doctors asked Ruth not to come to the hospital until she was completely over the effects of her illness. This did not occur until it was time for Shellie to come home. Being restricted from her daughter during this trying time was an additional burden Ruth didn't need.

Early each afternoon, I would arrive at the hospital and find Shellie safely in the arms of her loving grandmother. Ali would inform me of her general condition and the amount of fluids she had taken that morning. Then she would leave to go to our house and check on Ruth. Her selfless devotion to her family was a legacy that would endure for generations.

Upon Shellie's return home, the long road to recovery was begun once again with the aid of many people. But it was the courage and tenacious spirit of an unpretentious little girl that gave inspiration to us all.

The following year brought another gift of joy into our lives. Edward not only made our family complete, but also brought with him a buoyant and cheerful nature that would be a delight to all who knew him. His gregarious disposition would prove to be the glue that would hold our family together in years to come. Two boys and two girls, each two years apart.

The unnerving realization that, in the not too distant future, we would have four teenagers at one time made us want to enjoy their preadolescence even more.

David was now experiencing the opportunities and challenges of grade school. Each year new teachers, new friends, and increasing independence would bring with it memories of growth, provided by lessons hard learned.

These ensuing years would see Shellie continuing to progress at every level. She would walk again and regain limited use of her arm and hand. The constant and boundless smile would return and reflect her unlimited joy of life.

Amanda and Edward would develop a unique and unfaltering bond between them where each would take pride and delight in the success of the other.

These were happy years for Ruth and me, a time when we would grow through the responsibilities of parenthood, and our children would experience the carefree joys of youth. Through the stability and rewards of work, we would be able to buy our first home for our family. Through years of study and prayer, we would learn that this family unit could last forever.

Eventually, I was recalled to Western Airlines which, two years later, would result in our moving to Salt Lake City. While leaving one family in California, we were going to another in Utah. It's strange how often life can bring us full circle. Throughout my youth, I had benefited from the loving care of my gracious mother. Now it became our blessing to return the favor.

A new decade would bring with it a different landscape for our family. Who could foretell the challenges and achievements to come? Would there be more triumphs than tragedy? I have often been accused of being instinctively naive, a childish fault explained most recently by my best and lifelong friend. Through an insightfully accurate statement, he said, "You have always looked at things the way they should be, instead of the way they really are." However true this observation may be, I have found in my life that it is often the way we envision things that result in the way they ultimately become.

SEVEN

Many Different Mountains

We had decided to try to make our physical move to Salt Lake City as much of a vacation as possible. With most everything we owned packed in the center section of a large moving van, we loaded the balance of items into our station wagon and El Camino pickup. Once the remaining space was filled with two adults, four children, several finches, one large goldfish, and one small goldfish, there barely seemed to be enough room left inside the cars to change your mind. This looked like the Eyre family version of "The Grapes of Wrath."

After spending Edward's fourth birthday with my sister and brother-in-law on their ranch just south of Red Bluff, California, we proceeded on small, two-lane highways to the real mid point of our trip, Reno, Nevada. Following an evening of face painting at Circus-Circus and a restless night in a no star hotel, we awoke that morning to the sad realization that one of us had not survived the trip. The large goldfish, "Jaws," was alive and well, but his small counterpart had succumbed to all the excitement or altitude sickness and had died a rather ignominious death. A brief funeral service was held in the bathroom and then it was off, once again, on our pilgrimage to the new world.

Shellie and I were in the El Camino as we followed Ruth and Company along Interstate 80 through north central Nevada. I had only one person asking me if we were almost there yet, while

Ruth had three. The stops at Winnemucca and Battle Mountain were as much for sanity's sake as they were for bathroom breaks. By late afternoon, we stopped in Wendover, Nevada or Utah, depending on what side of the street you were on, where we decided to change cars. From there I would lead the charge across the Great Salt Lake Desert. It took only a few miles for me to appreciate the quiet conversation I had been enjoying with Shellie. This section of highway may represent one of the longest, straightest, most boring stretches of road on the entire Interstate system. However, as night began to fall and with less than one hundred miles remaining to Salt Lake City, that boredom would quickly convert to disquieting tension as we drove into the worst rainstorm I had ever experienced. Mile after mile my eyes would dart from the nearly invisible road ahead to the rear view mirror to ensure that Ruth was still safely behind us. Even with the windshield wipers going at full speed, they could not contend with the intensity of the downpour. The sound of children's voices had been quieted by the frightening noise of water splashing underneath the car and the barrage of thunder that followed each explosion of lightning. I could easily imagine that Ruth must have shared the conversion of the ever-present question, "Are we ever going to get there?" to, "Do we really want to go there?" It wasn't until we were in the safety of our high-rise hotel room in downtown Salt Lake that we could relax and look out over a city, witnessing the awesome display and power of Mother Nature.

The night provided time for the passage of the storm and a long awaited rest. The tension of the previous day's drive had been erased as the sunlight began to filter through the shades of the crowded room. Each of us began to move about in our individual routines until Ruth pulled back the drapes from the large window and flooded the room with the morning's brilliance. Whatever had been presently occupying us became secondary as we were all quietly drawn to the window and the panorama it provided. Looking directly south, the entire city seemed to expand before us. The Oquirrh Mountains to the west and the Wasatch Range to the east gave a feeling of resolute endurance to the valley below. The few remaining clouds provided a stark contrast to the clarion sky. For a few private moments, each of us seemed transfixed by what we were seeing with our eyes and imagining in our minds. I quickly noticed a Delta Airlines 727 as it gracefully descended along its final approach path. I could only wonder if the last two letters in its registration were WA. Six months prior, Delta had completed its purchase of Western Airlines. Few signs remained of this once proud company that had now flown into the history books. I doubted if any of the others had even noticed the airplane for we were all engrossed in our individual thoughts. Though the scene may be familiar, a resident views it differently than does a tourist.

I could only suspect that Ruth was visualizing the challenges of setting up a new house and getting acquainted with a new neighborhood. David, Amanda, and Edward must have been wondering about leaving the security of familiar surroundings and approaching the uncertainty of new friends and different schools. A smile came over my face as I thought that Shellie must have been questioning what in the world was going on. And yet I knew that, because of her accepting nature, she would easily take it all in stride.

Little attention was given to organization or detail as we quickly packed our things in anticipation of the short drive to Grandma's house. Once there, the kids were out of the car and through the front door before Ruth and I could collect a few small bags from the car.

As we approached the house, Mom descended the few front steps and welcomed us with outstretched arms. While still holding onto the bags, I awkwardly leaned forward as we exchanged kisses along with an affectionate greeting. But as I stepped aside to allow her access to Ruth I witnessed a markedly different scene. Ruth had placed the bags on the ground beside her and stepped forward to permit a sincere and uninhibited embrace. Although I initially regretted not showing the same thoughtfulness, I quickly became aware of the special nature of this moment. The images of a contrasting emotional experience, with uncanny similarities and yet painful differences, filled my mind. Just four days prior, Ruth had stood near the front steps of her parents' home, encircled in her mother's arms. She had always felt that there was a "oneness" about her mother and father, just as they had always felt about themselves, but the heartache of this tender farewell would remain individually with each of them. As the impression of the three of them faded back into the present and my focus returned to that of my mother and Ruth, I could sense that my father was there also, just slightly out of view.

Having always been grateful for the loving relationship Ruth had formed with my parents and knowing how important it was to my mother to have family near her again, I had somehow failed to appreciate this same need in Ruth. With her eyes gently closed, I saw a sense of peace and comfort, once again, come over her face, a look, I realized, I had not enjoyed seeing for quite some time. As they withdrew just far enough to look into each other's eyes, I witnessed that silent transfer of understanding only women share. Many of Ruth's concerns had just dissolved into my mother's perceptiveness. Even though I could never emulate this, I could at least appreciate it.

Though we were looking forward to our furniture arriving and getting settled into the house we had leased nearby, the three days we spent with my mother were filled with our children swimming in her community pool and her acquainting us with local stores, streets, and freeways. To escape the late afternoon heat of these August days, we would pack a light dinner, and within twenty minutes, be in one of the beautiful canyons for a relaxing evening picnic.

The magnificent Wasatch Range is close enough to be imposing; yet it also renders a sense of awesome nobility. As you enter one of its narrow valleys and ascend up the winding road, you never get the feeling that you are taming the mountain, but within its serenity, you sense that it is taming you.

Following dinner, we would sit at the picnic table and watch as the kids played in the cool mountain stream. It was as if we were all becoming reacquainted with our common relationship with nature. These evenings also afforded Ruth and me the time for long, quiet conversations with a woman who had nurtured me even before I was born.

I had always found my mother to be a person of unwavering principles, someone with interesting and informed opinions and a willingness to express them. Yet at the same time, she was more interested in listening to the opinions of others. Her love for her family seemed to transcend distance and time.

Yet, as I watched her gaze at our children at play, I could see in her face the joy of the present and in her eyes the vision of the distant future.

We had leased a beautiful home in a neighborhood that we could only hope to afford to live in someday. I was only twenty minutes from the airport and we were only five minutes away from my mother's house. Not having to commute hundreds of miles to work made my job so much more enjoyable and afforded much more time at home. The daily conversations Ruth was able to have with my mother gave her the sense of extended family that was so important and made the transition so much easier. Through our involvement in church and schools, we quickly came to know many of the people in our neighborhood. There were lots of kids in this community of relatively new homes, and within a matter of days, there seemed to be a myriad of new faces in the house and yard and an abundance of new names to learn.

School started just days after we moved in, and David and Amanda attended the elementary school just three blocks away. Edward went to a preschool at a neighbor's house nearby, and Shellie began her second grade special education class at Longview Elementary. It's always amazing how quickly children can adjust to new surroundings and Shellie was no exception. Her teacher was just out of college and was filled with enthusiasm and energy, while in the process of gaining the quiet confidence which comes only from experience. Ruth and I met with her early in the year to work out the mandated IEP (Individual Education Program). These meetings were often not only attended by Shellie's teacher, but by her occupational and speech therapists, the teacher with whom she would be mainstreamed, and other appropriate administrative personnel. We had become familiar with these twice-yearly meetings and looked forward to agreeing upon mutually established goals for Shellie's school year. This was an extension of the wonderfully effective early intervention programs that had such a significant influence on her educational progress.

We had encouraged Shellie to be involved in all of the activities like every other child her age. We found it equally important to discipline her as we would any of our other children. It was during this process that we were able to witness the glory of Shellie learning to do so many things for and by herself. She was never doubtful of her abilities or made to feel that there was any reason why she shouldn't be able to reach her goals. During these early school years, she was acquiring many skills and discovering so many things that added to her joy of life. Shellie was learning now, but in the not too distant future, she would be teaching and influencing many others.

The following years would see our children continuing to grow through their individual experiences, the purposeful direction provided by dedicated teachers, and the influence of strong family values. The elementary school years seem to be a time where parents and educators can recognize the strengths and weaknesses of their children at an early age and still have the time and opportunity to influence and provide proper guidance. These are such critical years when children form habits, values, and morals which will be the basis for their individual character and disposition for much of their lives. Parents seem to travel on an influential sign wave throughout a child's life. There is a time, in these younger, formative years, where the mother and father are normally thought to be relatively intelligent human beings. This opinion often diminishes during the junior high and high school years where outside influences can have a major impact on a youth trying to discover his place in the universe. Thankfully, this "out of phase" condition normally returns to some form of harmonious rhythm as the cycle becomes complete, and the parent and child once again appreciate their commonalities. But for now, Ruth and I could enjoy these preadolescent years.

Changes were taking place rapidly in all our lives. As I became qualified on a different airplane, Ruth became president of the PTA, and we were able to buy a home just three blocks away from where we had been living. However, Shellie's timetable was somewhat different than the rest of ours. For her, changes and advancements came at a slower pace. She seemed to enjoy every moment of every day, as we tended to look back over the week with only a glance.

I have often thought of a beautifully poignant statement made by our niece, Kelly, to her mother shortly after Shellie was born. Though still a preteen herself, after Mary had explained Shellie's condition to her, she said, "Ruth and Ted will just be able to enjoy her as a child much longer than normal." The accuracy of that tender observation has become a wonderful reality.

Shortly after Shellie changed schools in the fourth grade, I had a rare occasion to stop by Liberty Elementary. Without Ruth to show me where Shellie's class was, I went directly to the office for directions. There were several adults and one student in the small room as I entered through the opened door. With the interruption of someone not familiar, the conversation stopped and all eyes were on me. Somewhat uncomfortably I said, "Excuse me. I'm looking for my daughter's classroom; her name is Shellie Eyre ..."

Fortunately, I was interrupted by one of the secretaries before I had a chance to embarrass both them and myself by spelling out our last name. "Oh, Shellie. She's in Caroline Bruce's room. Go out of the office, turn left, go down to the end of the hall, turn right, and you will find her room just three doors down on the left." As I was trying to rehearse these directions as quickly as I could in my mind, the man standing adjacent to the desk turned and walked toward me with his hand outstretched.

"Good morning. I'm Mr. Bateman, the principal. It's nice to meet you and a pleasure to have Shellie in our school." I cordially thanked him and tried to express how I knew she would enjoy attending here, but I was reluctant to engage in a longer conversation for fear of forgetting the sequence of directions to her class.

As I departed the doorway, the turn to the left was the only thing I was sure of. Thankfully, I spotted a gentleman at the end of the hall who, by what he was doing, was obviously the janitor. What better person to ask for continuing directions? Approaching him with a smile, I inquired, "Could you tell me where the special education classroom is?"

Being slightly shorter and somewhat smaller in build than I, he looked at me quizzically, and while leaning back and tilting his head, inquired, "Are you Shellie's dad?" I was stunned for a moment, wondering how he would know that. Could it be that Shellie was the only new student and that he was familiar with all the other parents? No, that couldn't be it, but I thought I had better reply before I took more time to consider other possibilities.

My smile had changed to a puzzled grin as I responded, "Yes."

"Oh, she's in Mrs. Bruce's classroom, straight down the hall on the left. The one with the door opened." Even after I thanked him, I continued to look at him for just a moment, and then slowly turned to walk down the hall. While still trying to figure out how he could have guessed who I was, I realized that, throughout my usual day, I only took time to meet people, while Shellie, on the other hand, took time to *know* them. The janitor, Butch, would remain friends with our family for many years after Shellie had left that school. I was only beginning to appreciate the long lasting effect she had on people.

The years at Liberty Elementary were an exceptional time for all of us. There were the physical, occupational, and speech therapists who were involved in Shellie's continued development, special classmates who would remain friends throughout her school age years, teachers like Mrs. Iverson in whose class Shellie was mainstreamed, and others who went far beyond what was merely required of them by organizing and coaching a Special Olympic team. Through the efforts of Lorie Henderson and others, Shellie had the joy of competing in the summer Special Olympics at a major university to the south of us, in winter competition at the ski resorts close to our home, and in gymnastic games during the fall. She proudly displayed the ribbons and medals in her bedroom for years after she left that wonderful school.

But it was her teacher, Caroline Bruce, that introduced Shellie to the possibilities of reading, the satisfaction of completing challenging work, and quite simply, the joy of learning. I wonder if that teacher ever really knew how much we appreciated her wonderfully positive attitude and how she always emphasized what

Shellie *could* accomplish while never mentioning what she *couldn't*. Throughout our many years of schooling, we may encounter dozens of instructors, but only a few stand out because of the rare ability they have to uncover that something that makes us feel special. Caroline Bruce, room 14B, was one such teacher.

We had lived in our new home for over two years now and were getting to the point where fewer neighbors were still referring to it by the name of the previous owners. We had nearly completed a good deal of remodeling with all of its associated disarray, and I was looking forward to ending the world's largest do-it-yourself project. Ruth was beginning to believe that someday we might live in something other than a construction zone. It was a large five-bedroom house, and we soon learned that the size of the mess you can make is only limited by the number of rooms you have.

David was now beginning junior high school with all of its accompanying adjustments, Shellie was ending her grammar school years, and Amanda and Edward were attending a private school in hopes of developing their strengths and improving any academic weaknesses. This was a time when things were running relatively smoothly and only necessary adjustments were required by anticipated changes.

Fall was in the air with all of its associated colors, crisp cool days, and afternoon breezes. This is a transitional period where one day you are in a short-sleeved shirt and the next day in your favorite sweater. Or that median time where you no longer need the lawn mower, but can't bring yourself to uncover the snow blower. Increasingly, Ruth and I were beginning to feel that winter was the price you had to pay for the beautiful spring, summer, and falls that we enjoyed so much.

The day was progressing through its normal routine with the kids in school and both of us working through our mental checklists of things to accomplish before 100% of our time was demanded by 400% more people. We looked forward to noon when we could come together for a quiet lunch and a lot of conversation containing things of little importance. Ruth was preparing two sandwiches as I saw the mailman working his way down our street. The timing was perfect. He would arrive at our house just as I arrived at the mailbox and lunch would be ready when I had returned with today's edition of bills and baloney. Returning to the house, I noticed what a beautiful red color our hedge had become and how it contrasted with the browning of the lawn. I made a mental note to drain the sprinkler system before it was too late.

In the center of our kitchen is an island that not only is the most convenient place to prepare food, but also serves as the central meeting place in the house. As Ruth turned to get the glasses out of the cupboard behind her, I laid the mail on the counter top between us and began to make two piles, one for letters and one for litter. Uttering some nonessential comment about each piece, I stopped as I noticed a rather familiar envelope. "That's strange," I said as I looked over the address for a second time.

Ruth placed the empty glasses down and questioned my puzzled look. "What's that?" she inquired.

"It's a letter from the Lucile Salter Packard Children's Hospital."

"Who in the world is that?" she asked.

"That's the children's part of Stanford Hospital where Shellie had her operation. We receive a letter from them every year soliciting a contribution and I always send one in, but that was just last month. Maybe they didn't get it, and this is just a follow up." I placed the letter off to the side, not delegating it to either of the two piles in front of me. As I continued to sort through what remained, Ruth slowly picked up the letter and opened it without my noticing.

Shortly after she began reading, she interrupted my screening process with a soft but serious tone. "Ted...this is no letter about a contribution."

Now she had my attention. "What is it?" I could tell by her lack of answer that I should wait until she was finished reading before I asked again. Upon completion, she removed her right hand from the letter and placed it on the counter as if to steady herself. At the same time, she raised her head and looked me in the eyes, and while not saying a word, offered me the letter. Trying unsuccessfully to read her face before anything else, I slowly retrieved the single page and began to quickly scan the message. I had only made it past the first few lines when my head shot up, our eyes met, and I blurted out the word, "AIDS."

Ruth's entire upper body instantly tensed up as she quickly shut her eyes and said, "Just...read the letter." As her eyes opened, mine lowered to the now trembling piece of paper in my hand. I laid it down on the top of the island and steadied myself by placing a hand on each side of it. This time I knew better than to quickly scan the words as I deliberately made my way from line to line. While I was reading to myself, Ruth slowly turned away and walked over to the kitchen table and pulled out her chair. The carefully prepared lunch was now totally unimportant.

The letter went on to state that, since a 1983 Public Health Service recommendation, potential blood donors at risk of HIV infection have been asked not to donate blood. Since 1985, all donated blood has been tested for evidence of HIV (human immunodeficiency virus). All blood found to contain evidence of HIV infection is discarded. Currently in the United States, there is only a very small chance of infection with HIV through a blood transfusion. However, since Shellie had surgery in 1979 and had received blood prior to these preventative measures, it was incumbent upon us to have her tested as soon as possible to determine if she had the disease known as Acquired Immunodeficiency Syndrome, or AIDS.

The letter continued to inform us that this was a simple blood test that could be performed by our daughter's current pediatrician. Leaving the letter on the counter top, I quietly walked over to my chair at the end of the table and sat down adjacent to Ruth. Her stare was focused on her hands that were clasped tightly together and resting on the table.

Not knowing just what to say and not wanting to say the wrong thing, I decided silence was appropriate for the moment. As much as I wanted a dialogue to begin, I didn't want to be the one to initiate it. After all, Ruth had had a few more minutes to think this over, and I wanted her to express her feelings and set the tone for our conversation. Slowly, I raised my right arm and placed my hand on top of her delicately woven fingers. As I did, she raised her head and our eyes met, each of us thinking while, at the same time, trying desperately to read the thoughts of the other. Wanting her to say something, I raised my eyebrows and right hand at the same time as if to plead with my actions instead of my words. Slowly, she drew a deep breath. Holding it just momentarily, she exhaled the words, "I don't believe she has it. I just don't think Shellie has AIDS."

With that, the dam broke. I could express everything that I had not taken the time to think through yet. "Neither do I, and the reason I don't is because Shellie has been so healthy. Sure, she gets a cold, sure she gets the flu, but she gets over them just like everyone else, which is further proof that her immune system is just fine. It's been over ten years since she received those transfusions. We would have noticed something by now. I don't think you can be infected with HIV for that long and not have full blown AIDS by now. Besides, what are the chances..." As Ruth closed her eyes, I could tell it was time for me to stop and let the dust settle.

After an embarrassingly quiet minute or two, Ruth said in a more businesslike tone, "We have to call Dr. Metcalf and get Shellie in for a blood test. If you'll look up the number, I'll make the call." Ruth politely refused the offer to have the doctor call her back and was put on hold for an amazingly short while. After explaining the contents of the letter, an appointment was made for the following afternoon. I realized I had a three-day trip and would be leaving that morning, but taking the sample wasn't nearly as important as receiving the results.

The next day, shortly after I left for the airport, Ruth and Shellie left for the doctor's office. After going over the letter and discussing the procedure with Ruth, Dr. Metcalf drew the blood sample. He then informed her he would let us know the results when the tests were concluded, which normally requires seven to eight days.

We had been over this ground before, as the memories flooded back of other times that we had waited, worried, and prayed. Armed with a bit more maturity, it was still difficult not to think of the consequences both day and night. On an unspoken yet mutually accepted agreement, Ruth and I chose not to continue any extended speculation on something that no one else in the family, including Shellie, knew anything about. While counting down the days, I couldn't help but recall the analogous feelings we had experienced just ten years earlier when, again, Shellie's well being was at stake. I remembered also, the anxiety of eight and six years ago as we waited for the amniocentesis results from Amanda and Edward. For every different mountain that you climb, there must be a corresponding number of valleys.

A week had passed by and I was outside working around the back of the house, trying to prepare the bushes for the snow that was soon to arrive. Through the window above me, I heard the phone ring but chose not to run inside. Instead, I held my breath for a heartbeat or two as the unremitted prayer echoed in my head. Following the sound of the patio door sliding along its track, Ruth came out on the single step. Before locating me, I could see no joy or relief in her face. As our eyes met, it seemed as though any discernible emotion had been covered by shock as she simply said, "The results came back positive." Without exhaling, the air had seemed to escape my lungs. My mind went blank, as numbness consumed both emotion and thought. As I stood motionless, Ruth approached me, obviously wanting to be closer before she continued. "Dr. Metcalf says this test is not definitive. In fact, I think the word he used was inconclusive. He says that there are numerous false positives and that we need to do more tests to verify these results. He suggests..."

"No! No more tests! Inconclusive is good enough for me."

Ruth looked at me in disbelief as I continued: "We're not putting Shellie through any more tests. We're not putting ourselves through another week of waiting for some lab results. No! I'm not going to do it! We have our own test results. Ten years of observation, that's what we have. As far as I'm concerned, Shellie does not have AIDS. End of chapter! We're in the index! Inconclusive means undetermined. Not definitive means not reliable. We're not going to do this!"

"Ted, stop this. And what do you mean 'we'? Don't you think I have something to say about this! Once again, you're talking before you're thinking."

"Don't tell me I'm talking before I'm thinking. I've been thinking about this for twenty-four hours a day for a solid week. No more tests and that's it!"

As I stormed back toward the house, Ruth turned, and in a voice loud enough to carry beyond the yard shouted, "Well, that's a real mature, constructive attitude." I froze in my steps. My jaws closed just slightly tighter than my eyes. Slowly, I turned around, and in total silence, we stared at each other with unfamiliar contempt. I realized this was the first time we had ever raised our voices at each other, the first time we had not agreed on a course of action in support of each other. This was foreign territory, but the distance between us was far greater than the twenty feet that could be measured across the ground. It would be some time before this bridge would be rebuilt.

Returning to the house, I went straight for the garage and drove away, not knowing or caring where I went. The more I drove, the more guilty I felt. I was torn between my total resolve in this matter and wanting to be with Ruth. I had not helped the situation; I had just created another problem. Even so, as I turned the car around, I knew I could go back to the house but not back on my convictions. The atmosphere in the house that evening was cool, to say the least. And even though each of our children could not discern the cause, somehow they knew it was better to speculate than to ask. The fact that I was leaving the following morning on another trip seemed like a good idea to everyone.

It seems almost uncanny that, when your mind is on a particular subject, you hear and see more evidence of it than ever before. This, I'm sure, must simply be due to the fact that you are more in tune to its existence. But throughout my time away, I was constantly reminded of the one thing I was trying to deny. When I turned on the radio, there would be a news story about AIDS. When I opened the paper, there would be an article about medicines that could slow the affects of the HIV virus. In my hotel room during the evening, there never failed to be a report of it on the nightly news. By the second day, I found myself conscientiously avoiding any sources of news. I couldn't live like this for very long. Upon my return home, though our conversations were much calmer than at first, the gulf between us was still as wide.

Ruth thought it was imperative that we have the additional tests completed as soon as possible, so that if the results were confirmed, we could notify the school, our neighbors, doctors etc. I knew that what she was advocating was the responsible thing to do, but I couldn't accept the total disruption this would mean for our family. I still wanted to hide under the protection of the word "inconclusive." I was alarmed to find myself repeating so many of the phases that we had traversed so many years ago: shock, disbelief, denial. Finally, we had progressed to the last and most positive phase. This was to realize we could not change Shellie's condition. We had come to accept it and were united in our efforts to make the most of it. Had I not learned anything? Was I going to have to work my way painfully through this labyrinth again? Still, the chaos and disorder I imagined that would come upon our children and us frightened me all the more. I knew Ruth was right, wanting to protect the welfare of others, but as unbelievable as it might sound, the depth of my denial had caused me to overlook the single most important factor.

It wasn't until the third day of my second trip away that I was shocked back into reality. As I sat in the cockpit just prior to our last leg home, I became aware that the departure time had come and gone and we still hadn't boarded the passengers. Inquiring as to the nature of the delay, I was informed that they were working on something back in the cabin. I unbuckled my seat belt and went back to investigate. There I found two mechanics, working at the base of some seats. I inquired, "Can't they be fixed, or just locked in the upright position?"

One of the mechanics looked up at me and answered, "The seats aren't broken. There was a guy sitting here with a bad case of AIDS, coming here for some treatment. He and his medical assistant were using these two seats, so we're replacing them." He had no idea of the impact of what he had just said. They weren't changing the cushions, they were removing the seats!

Any questions I had about the hysteria surrounding this condition had been answered. Not wanting to show my reaction, I quickly turned away and continued back towards the cockpit. I stopped halfway through the empty first class section. Out of all he had just said, one word kept repeating itself in my mind. *Treat-*

ment. He was coming here for medical treatment. My Lord, where had I been? If there was any chance that Shellie did have AIDS, then the most important thing was to get her help. I had not heard Ruth because I had refused to listen. Was I more concerned about the possible disruption of the social lives of our other children than I was about Shellie's welfare? Had I given more consideration to reputations and liabilities than I had to her long-term health? How could I have such strong opinions about a condition I knew so little about?

I knew now that we had to get the follow up tests done, but I still desired to find a way that would accommodate some of my fears?

Upon my arrival home, Ruth could sense the softening of my disposition. She was anxious for the harmony to return, but knew I would have to concede in my own way and time.

The following morning began with its normal routine of everyone getting ready at once. The idea that you can never be too thin or too rich should be combined with *you can never have too many bathrooms.* By eight o'clock, the only thing that exceeded the peace and quiet was the mess that had been left behind.

Normally, Ruth disliked my reading at the table, but our morning ritual of sharing the newspaper as we ate breakfast was the singular exception. As I continued to scan the headlines to find an article of interest, my eyes passed over a small ad at the bottom of the page. Something within it had caught my attention and my focus returned to read it more carefully. "Take the test and take control. National HIV testing day. Free, confidential HIV testing." The lettering was of various sizes, and even though the word "free" was much larger, it was the following word that I continued to stare at. "Confidential." There was my answer. Quickly, I folded the paper so I could place it next to Ruth on the table. Pointing to the ad, I stated, "There it is. Confidential testing, Friday and Saturday. That's today and tomorrow. We can take Shellie down there, have the test done, and if they come back negative, no one will ever know that we even went through all of this. If it comes back positive, just the two of us will be able to sit down, privately, and discuss our course of action."

Ruth readily agreed, not caring what concessions had to be made, but only that the tests were done. I called the telephone number in the ad to insure that this would be the more comprehensive, definitive series of tests. The lady assured me that there would be three individual screening tests. Two ELISA tests and one referred to as a Western Blot Test. No appointment was necessary and the center was open from 9:00 A.M. to 6:00 P.M.

That was it. Ruth would have her test results in seven to ten days and I would have the confidentiality to give us time to think it all out. The decision was made that I would take Shellie in the following morning.

As we drove up the wide, tree-lined street, the colors of autumn were everywhere. The sky was crystal clear, and as we passed the city park, the job of picking up all those leaves put my own task in the front yard in proper perspective.

Shellie was glad to be out on such a beautiful day, and because, over her short life, she had been to so many doctors and had numerous operations, one more blood test was of little concern. As we drove into the parking lot of the Public Health Center, just to the southeast of the downtown area, no inquiry was made as to why she had never been here before. We held hands as we entered the room and proceeded to the reception area. Shellie was too short to look over the tall counter and, instead, became occupied with looking at the dozen or so people sitting around the waiting room. After explaining why I was there, I was handed a purple sheet of paper that had to be completed prior to the tests being administered. The upper left hand corner contained several peel-off strips with the same five-digit number.

As we sat down and I looked over the paper, I noticed that nearly everyone else in the room had a similar purple form. An uncomfortably nervous feeling came over me as I tried to avoid all the things going through my mind by concentrating on the questions. The only things on the paper that could indicate the person's identity were the numbers at the top and a question regarding your zip code. Much of the rest was a "risk factor" sheet, asking many questions that didn't seem to apply to Shellie. Most were inquiries as to work place exposure and the type and frequencies of sex you had been involved in. The letters N/A went into a number of spaces.

After waiting about forty-five minutes, our number was called and we were led to a small private room. Very little conversation ensued as the purple form was looked over and the blood was drawn. The nurse then informed us to call the clinic after seven days to see if the results for this test number were in. On the drive home, Shellie seemed occupied with the activities occurring outside the car, and I was caught up in the silence of my thoughts.

On the morning of the seventh day, we called the clinic and inquired about the test results for number 15670. We were informed that they were complete and we could come in at any time to discuss the results. Obviously, nothing was more important on our calendar that day.

The temperature was much cooler than the day Shellie and I had driven up 7th East and fewer leaves now remained on the trees. As we turned off the car in the nearly empty lot of the health center, no words were exchanged. Ruth and I just looked into each other's eyes and silently hoped for the best.

Upon approaching the counter, I noticed that there were only two or three people in the waiting room. We told the receptionist that we were here for the results and gave her the five-digit number. She told us to wait in the hall and we would be called momentarily. We had barely sat down on the two available chairs before a woman approached us, dressed in everyday business attire. She directed us to a small room down the hall, and once we were inside and seated, she closed the door behind her but remained standing in front of it.

As she took just a moment to look at both of us, she then inquired, "Which one of you is 15670?" Ruth looked puzzled, as she was not as familiar with the number as I was. I quickly responded that neither of us were, but it was our daughter who had received the test. She looked somewhat shocked, but then stated in a very direct voice. "Well, I can't give these test results to you. They can only be given to the person who took the test."

Now we were the ones that were shocked. The tension and emotions had been welling up in us for seven days, and now we were going to be denied these results. I was momentarily too stunned to talk. Ruth quickly protested, with her voice beginning to shake, "You don't understand. Our daughter is only ten years old. She doesn't realize what this is all about."

But before Ruth could continue, the nurse interrupted, "I'm sorry, but you'll have to understand that I could have my medical license revoked if I give these confidential results to anyone other than the person who took the test. I'm sorry, but that is the way the program is set up." Ruth could no longer contain her emotions as she broke forth with tears streaming down her face.

I could feel my entire body temperature rise at once, but trying to disguise my deepening anger, I took a long breath and continued a petition for common sense to prevail. "Look, our daughter has Down syndrome. She received this blood transfusion ten years ago. She's not capable of understanding the implications here. We are not only her parents, but the ones who will have to make the decisions in this matter."

As I stopped to catch my breath, Ruth looked up into the woman's eyes, and with impassioned concern, simply implored, "Please,...please."

The silence was as thick as the tension in the room. Slowly the nurse released the folder she had been holding next to her chest. After looking its contents over briefly, her eyes returned to Ruth and me. She shook her head back and forth in a negative response and then quietly said, "I can't tell you the specific results of these tests...but I can tell you that your daughter will be all right... she'll be just fine."

Although a weight had been lifted off my shoulders, I felt as if all strength had left me. My head fell forward just as Ruth buried her face in her hands. The tears of despair had now been replaced with ones of thankfulness and joy. After a brief moment to regain our composure, and following an expression of gratitude, we passed through the door, turned to the right and continued down the hall. Through the glass of the large double doors I could see clouds forming in the west and the nearly barren trees blowing in the wind. As I leaned forward to open the door for Ruth, a large blast of cold air rushed across our faces. Stopping for just a moment, she slowly turned towards me, and where there would normally have been a negative comment about the impending weather, only a heartwarming smile was exchanged. The winter was going to be far more tolerable this year.

EIGHT

Shining Examples

To many of us, changes do not come easily. They are more often looked upon as challenges rather than opportunities. When confronted with such, it is only natural to try to analyze the situation, evaluate the positives and negatives, and choose a course of action. Frequently, this can be a very intimidating, if not a painful process. More often than not, the anguish brought on by the fear of something not previously experienced and a tendency to emphasize the negative, result in anxiety which is mostly self-induced. I believe Mark Twain once said, "The majority of things I feared the most, never happened." The disconcerting fact is that many of these changes are brought about by something we had no control over. The only thing we can control is how we react to them.

The older we get, the more tendency we have to feel that the challenges or changes we face today are far greater or of more importance than those of our youth. In reality, the apprehension of a twelve-year-old facing the first day of seventh grade is every bit as real and important as the concerns of a parent who may face the loss of his job. The ramifications may be in direct proportion to our stage in life, but the degree of seriousness remains the same.

On the morning of the first day of classes for the 1992-1993 school year, I was in Calgary, Alberta, Canada. Even though we were more than seven hundred miles apart, the fact that we were in the same time zone made me look at my watch repeatedly throughout the morning. I tried to visualize the excited yet chaotic scene that must have been unfolding at home. As I showered and shaved in the quiet stillness of my hotel room, I could only imagine the demands being put on Ruth. I could envision Amanda pleading for help with her hair, Shellie trying desperately to figure out how to plug-in the toaster without toasting herself, and a loud cry from the laundry room as Edward hopelessly looked for a pair of matching socks. The traveling demands of my career sometimes have their advantages.

At the same time our crew left for the airport, Ruth's crew would be dispersing to three different schools. David was beginning his ninth grade year and ending a rewarding season of football. Amanda and Edward were starting the fifth and third grades, respectively, and Shellie was commencing a whole new career in junior high school.

As we leveled off at our cruise altitude and as the tasks that were necessary during the take off and climb were now behind us, we each settled into the reduced work load of monitoring the progress of the flight for the next hour or so. My thoughts quickly returned to our four children and the individual ordeals they were experiencing on this late summer morning. I marveled at how Ruth was able to successfully choreograph this sequence of demands, day after day, year after year. As with any couple at this point in life, our primary concern was the continuing development and well being of our children. I sincerely believe that a parent is only as happy as their least happiest child. Thankfully, this was a time when Ruth and I were very happy. But the concern of how you can best influence and guide your children in the most positive way is always paramount.

It was this insecurity that I now found myself concentrating on. As we approached the boarder of Canada and the United States, I looked around the cockpit for a piece of scratch paper to write down some thoughts that had come to mind. It would be many years before I would share this simple poem with our children, and even though the verse may be quite weak, the feelings it left with me that morning were very strong.

Learned Man

Oh, that I was a man of wisdom,
    a man of letters and of words. One that
could express my inner most thoughts,
    without sounding too absurd. To be able to
 teach, influence and inspire
    those who mean so much to me.
That they too could know, that you truly become
    exactly what you choose to be.

Every child has been told that the world
    is what you make it. But for many, a few
failures or shattered dreams,
    make it more convenient just to fake it.

And yet around us we know of people
    who always overcome, Those who
make the most of life,
    not the many, just the some. Which of
those two types will I become?
    Who is it that could say?
 I can, that's who,
    my future starts today.

As my thoughts returned to our children, I knew that three of them would most likely have to learn these lessons of life through the trials of experience. But one, Shellie, seemed to be blessed at birth with this positive instinct. I believe it to be a heavenly gift, given to but a chosen few.

The junior high school years are thought, by most people, to be that intermediate time when we expand on the elementary knowledge acquired during the grade school years and preparatory to a time when we will use that information in high school. My interpretation of these three periods of secondary education is a bit more basic. I have always felt that grade school was a time when you learn *how* to study, junior high school is when you learn *what* to study, and high school is when your learn *why* you study at all.

But for Shellie, things were not always so black and white. She tended to combine the how, what, and why into her own personal understanding at every phase of her life.

Few would argue that these teenage years are the quintessential period of acclimation and adjustment. However, for Shellie, her adaptability would prove to be one of her greatest advantages in life.

Of the two large junior high schools in our city, the one closest to our home, would be attended by all of our children with the exception of Shellie. Over the years, it had evolved from being a small high school to a building with many dissimilar additions. To find your way through its maze of hallways, elevators, and staircases, you needed a map equivalent to the visitor's guide at Disneyland.

For this reason, the decision was made to have the special education classes at Riverview Junior High instead of Hillcrest. Though it may have been farther away for some, at least it was built on one level.

Not going to your neighborhood school may have been seen as a disadvantage to most, but to Shellie it was an exciting opportunity to meet many other people she would not have known otherwise.

Here, through the work of her teacher, Sherrie Heaton and the acceptance of the administration and other instructors, she would realize the promised hope of "mainstreaming." Being given the freedom to join in every class from physical education to girls choir not only gave Shellie the joy of participation, but also gave her classmates the fortunate circumstances to discover that disabled children share the same emotions, desires, hopes, and dreams that they have. This integration emphasizes their similarities and minimizes their differences. In such an environment, both groups have an enhanced ability to achieve their greatest potential.

This was all made possible by a provision of the American Disabilities Act, Public Law 94-142, which was implemented in 1975. It required that a free and appropriate public education and related services be provided in the least restrictive environment for each student with a handicap through the age of 21. When the law was first introduced, it was met with a great deal of skepticism on the part of many teachers and administrators. They realistically and genuinely felt that their plate was full, that there would be minimal benefit for the disabled child in a "normal" classroom environment, and that the possible disruption of having to address the needs of these special students would infringe on precious classroom time. The concerns of these educators were perfectly legitimate, and many parents found that they had to fight to ensure that the law was implemented as planned. But over the course of time, previously held convictions were slowly transformed and school personnel came to recognize the benefits more than the impediments. In our case, we found Shellie's classmates to be supportive and helpful. They enjoyed the role of being the teacher and quickly became very comfortable and accepting toward the handicapped students. Of course, Shellie's disposition and loving nature had a great deal to do with her success in this endeavor. Whoever said, "attitude is everything," knew what they were talking about.

Shellie's activities outside of school included everything from summer girls' camp to competitive horseback riding and church league basketball. The latter was one of the finest examples of pure sportsmanship I had ever witnessed.

While the coaches honestly welcomed Shellie onto the team, it was her teammates who willingly included her into each practice and game. As her name was called to come off the bench and into the rotation, the cheers from the sidelines could not drown out the encouragement given to her by the rest of the team.

The shear thrill of participating seemed to overshadow any intimidation of not knowing the strategy or rules of the game. As one of her teammates would pull down a defensive rebound, play would nearly stop as she called out Shellie's name. The ball would be gently tossed underhanded and undisturbed to Shellie's waiting arms. An honest attempt at dribbling would be enough to satisfy the referees' interpretation of the traveling rule as Shellie continued down the floor. After carefully positioning herself in front of the basket and supporting the ball with her weakened left hand, the room would become strangely quiet as the ball arched its way toward the basket. Because of a seventy percent shooting average, more often than not, both teams and each set of coaches would jump to their feet as the ball fell through the hoop. After a series of "high fives" from opponents as well as teammates, the intensity of play would resume. Shellie would be the last one down the court as she smiled and waved to the cheering spectators.

I would marvel at this scene of compassion in the midst of competition and at the grace and maturity of those wonderful girls. However, in years to come, I would witness this display of sincere unselfishness on a far greater scale.

With junior high school now fondly remembered as a collection of wonderful experiences with friends and activities, Shellie began her high school years with the same optimistic enthusiasm with which she welcomed every other phase of her life. Only during the beginning portion of her first day at Murray High did she exhibit some uncharacteristic shyness. As the bell rang, indicating the end of the second period, the unharmonious sound of noisy confusion began to fill the hallway outside the classroom. Turning away from her scheduling notes, Kelli Kercher approached Shellie with an intuition gained from years of teaching experience. She knew the next statement would have to be said with a calculated degree of encouraging tactfulness. "Shellie, it's time to go to your next class." Looking up and over the top of her glasses, Shellie ponderously shook her head back and forth with uneasy apprehension. Pretending not to notice, Kelli continued, "Do you like to sing?" Shellie's eyes widened at the same time the motion of her head converted to an unqualified affirmative.

An exuberant "yes" dispelled any question that this was one of her favorite activities.

"Well, your next class is Girls' Choir and I'm sure Mr. Scott is waiting to meet you. I'll bet you already know some of the kids in that class. If you'll take my hand, I'll show you where the choir room is, okay?" No further encouragement was necessary, as the thought of being able to sing with a group of other students had overcome any fear or trepidation.

Once they were out in the hall, the advantage of Shellie going to a junior high school that was across town, while living in the neighborhood of the rival school, became immediately apparent. Kelli was amazed at the number of students that recognized and greeted Shellie by name. By the time they reached the choir room, she was forced to inquire, "How do you know so many of these kids?"

Shellie's voice was filled with renewed confidence, "I don't know, they're just my friends." As she entered the classroom and walked toward one of the empty chairs on the front row, she barely noticed Mr. Scott as she waved to those who were already seated and yelled, "Hi everybody!" The response was a mixture of acknowledgement of Shellie by name combined with accepting laughter as Shellie settled both into her seat and back into her element.

This particular class was a combination of two of the things Shellie enjoyed most in life: being with friends and music. But the year would be filled with other rewarding and exciting academic opportunities from modern dance to computers to religious studies. Every class would present unique challenges and difficulties which would be overcome by a positive attitude and a cheerful heart.

However, these attributes would be aided to a great extent by the "peer tutor" program in place at Murray High. Though not implemented by her teacher, Kelli Kercher, it was certainly enhanced by her efforts. It had become a fully accredited academic class, an elective under the social studies program. Students would receive .5 credits each semester for coming into the special education classroom and helping disabled class members with particular assignments or skills. There was homework involved and a requirement for two after-school activities. Hardly a weekend went by without one of these tutors calling to ask Shellie out to a movie or to go to the mall. We soon learned that many of these extra activities were going unreported for credit and were instead just volunteered from the heart. The class had grown, by word of mouth, to a point where all the slots were quickly filled. Students came to love working with the disabled while at the same time learning a great deal about themselves.

In every class, Shellie gained new friends for the simple reason that it was so natural for her to show her love for others. This affection would blossom into one of her first high school crushes on a handsome athlete in the junior class.

Cris Wilkinson lived only a few blocks from our house and we had been friends with his family since the first week of moving into the neighborhood. One afternoon early in the school year, I lightheartedly teased him about Shellie's newfound affection. He stated a theme that we would hear repeatedly throughout Shellie's high school years. With requited admiration, he responded, "Whenever I'm having a bad day, she can turn it all around with her infectious smile. Just being around her lifts my spirits." Once again, we were learning a valuable lesson from a young and unpretentious teacher. It's a simple formula that Shellie has employed for acquiring many sincere friends: *"It's hard not to like someone when you know they like you."*

This talent came easily and naturally to someone who looked upon each day with joyful anticipation. Shellie had become the thread of continuity in our family.

But due to the humbling effects of a simple extra chromosome, many things would be profoundly complex and difficult to master. Because of the crippling influences of her stroke, she would never be able to dance or play her guitar with the adeptness she would otherwise have had. But the talents of the heart were given to her as a gift from the Master of unconditional love. Somehow, Shellie instinctively knew that the reward came in giving her gifts back to others. Thoreau once said, "To affect the quality of the day, that is the highest of arts."

Following a wonderful family vacation to England where the kids were constantly thrilled with the sights of that beautiful country and occasionally terrorized by my attempt to drive on the wrong side of the road, we settled in for another exciting year of academia.

David was out of school, Shellie was beginning her junior year, and Amanda and Edward were attending the same junior high while continuing their unique relationship as brother and sister. The association they enjoyed reminded me so much of the bond between my sister Naomi and myself when we were growing up. Naomi always tried to include me in much the same way Amanda included Ed. Her friends were his friends also, and it always feels good and reassuring to have strong ties with those who are upper classmen.

Much of Shellie's class schedule would remain the same that year with a bit more emphasis put on independent living skills taught in her special education classroom. The peer tutor program would continue to attract quality people with the sincere interest of including these kids into all the school activities. For many students, this would be the first time that they would enjoy the enriching experience of taking a class for personal satisfaction and development rather than to receive credits toward graduation. For some, it would determine what course of study they would pursue after high school. But for all of them, it would impact the feelings of their heart forever.

Shellie became the first handicapped child to try out for her cheerleading booster squad. These forty girls were the Murray Spartan Peppers and would contribute greatly to the school spirit at football and basketball games. She loved wearing the uniform and being involved with the other girls. Initially, there was some administrative discussion about not allowing Shellie to attempt to make the team because of special considerations or liabilities, but once it was understood that the liabilities would be far greater if she were denied this opportunity, the path was suddenly made clear.

Their faculty advisor, Audra Kasparion, only equaled the support she received from the other girls. Great leaders set great examples and Audra did just that whether it was in academic classes or extra curricular activities. Some people just naturally know that everyone has something to contribute to the group as a whole when given the proper encouragement.

It was thrilling to all of us to see Shellie participate in such an integrated way. We, along with many others, came away from the games having been inspired by more than just the competition.

We had long been impressed with the sincere acts of kindness extended to Shellie by the students of this exceptional high school, but our expectations were exceeded one evening in early December of that year.

The house was decorated inside and out in anticipation of the coming holidays and we had just completed dinner when the doorbell rang. Ruth was first at the door and I was only a few steps behind, anticipating a neighbor or friend bringing something over for this special season. As I arrived at the entryway, I noticed Ruth talking with Sarah Martinsen, one of Shellie's peer tutors. She was holding in her hands a beautiful white teddy bear and a bag of candy kisses. My first thought was that she had brought this kind gift over for Shellie, but as I began to listen to the conversation, it became evident that this was not the intent of her visit. As I drew closer, both Ruth and I became aware that she was here merely to introduce someone else.

"Before you get Shellie, please let me explain that this invitation is sincere and from the heart. This is something that these two boys have wanted to do for some time." She was interrupted by Shellie coming down the stairs. Amanda also came into the room to see what was going on. After the girls had exchanged greetings, Sarah turned to wave at someone waiting in the car. Within just a few moments, standing next to Sarah was a very tall, extremely handsome young man.

Sarah continued," Shellie, you know Brett Kitchen, don't you? He was one of the star basketball players on our state championship team." Shellie's head was tilted back as far as it could go and her mouth was opened just slightly less than her eyes, but no acknowledgement could be formed. "He is here to ask you something." With that, Sarah handed the bear and candy to Brett as he took a step closer to Shellie and bent down.

In a soft and caring voice, Brett began, "There's a little note on the bear. Can I read it to you? It says 'I'd be beary happy if you would go to the Kissmas Dance with me!'" There was a short pause as everyone stood in total silence. Then Brett's long arms came forward as he presented the gift of the teddy bear and candy kisses to an awestruck recipient. Noting the opportunity for further explanation, he continued, "One of my best friends, Russ Thomson, is going to ask one of your best friends, Brittany Shaw, to the dance, and if you would like, we could double date. Maybe after the dance we could go out for some ice cream. Shellie, will you go with me to the dance?"

Her head shook up and down, but before she could say anything, Brett elaborated on the events of the upcoming evening. "It's a Christmas theme, and since the dress is casual, I thought it would be fun if we dressed alike. Maybe we could both wear jeans and I could bring you over a red turtleneck and I could wear a green one. What d' ya say?"

Finally Shellie found her voice but not her breath as she faintly exhaled, "Sounds good to me." My eyes drifted away from this tender scene to focus on Ruth and I noticed the tears forming in her eyes. I could see in the glow of her face a combination of emotions. How proud she was of this young man and how happy she was for Shellie. As I looked over at Amanda, her face also expressed the thrill of this exceptional moment.

Shellie barely touched ground during the following week as she asked each morning how many more days until Friday. The night of the dance found her in as much anxious, excited anticipation as any girl waiting the arrival of her first date.

Prior to this evening, she had always attended the school dances with her special education class as a group, but tonight would be different, far different.

The evening was progressing right on schedule with pictures being taken and the dance floor filled with hundreds of students enjoying the music and carefree conversation. To Shellie, it was a musical dream come true. The two of them had danced most of the dances together while enjoying the company of a large group of friends as the disc jockey searched for just the right song to continue the melodic continuity.

Brett, Shellie, Russ, and Brittany were in the center of the dance floor as the music from the song "My Girl" rolled out of the speakers. With everyone starting to dance around them, Brett and Russ looked at each other and said, "Let's do it." To the surprise of Shellie and Brittany, along with everyone else on the dance floor, these young men kneeled down on one knee, and while looking up at their surprised dates, began to sing every word of the song. In quiet amazement, all the other students stopped dancing and circled around the four spotlighted individuals. It quickly became obvious to all in the gymnasium that these two boys were not trying to draw attention to themselves, but to the two spellbound girls they honored. In doing so, they had captivated the hearts and touched the lives of all those who watched. They were demonstrating to anyone who might have questioned their motives that they were truly proud to be with these two angelic girls.

Those who described this act of selfless compassion to Ruth and me said it was the singular most emotional experience they could remember in high school. Brett and Russ did it to touch the hearts of two special girls, but they had no idea that they had touched and influenced the hearts and attitudes of the hundreds that watched in amazement. Through the strength of their character, they had altered the perspective of an entire student body. The effects of this exceptional moment would be felt for years to come.

Throughout the remainder of the year, Shellie was asked to every dance: the informal stomps, Spring Formal, and finally Junior Prom where she and her date were announced on the rotunda steps of the state capital building to thunderous applause. All of this was initiated by a loving peer tutor and a tall, handsome star athlete with a tender heart and a willingness to set the example.

Shellie's world would never be the same because, for the first time in her life, she had fallen in love.

NINE

What's in a Name

The senior year of high school is normally one of the most unforgettable times in a person's life. It is often a dichotomy of emotional feelings where you are caught between the realization of the finality of one phase of your life and the anxious anticipation of unseasoned independence. You have truly experienced the sensitivity of love and now must face the possibility of separation. The realization that you are now king of the hill is somewhat tempered with the knowledge that you must soon face the mountains of life. This last formal year of high school would not only be memorable for Shellie, but for the rest of our family as well.

Because of the willingness of Ruth to work as a parent coordinator for the pep club and encouragement from a number of others involved, Shellie was given the opportunity to enjoy a second year as a Spartan Pepper. Once again, the thrill of participating in each football and basketball game became something she looked forward to each week. The response we received from other parents made us come to know that they experienced the same feelings that we had while watching her add to the school spirit.

Amanda was now attending the same school as a sophomore and soon became aware of the feelings of the other students toward Shellie. But there was never a feeling of jealousy on her part, only a sense of pride in Shellie and all these incredible students who went out of their way to make sure she felt included. The two of them attended several classes together and Amanda came to esteem her role as Shellie's younger sister. However, the benefits worked both ways as Amanda brought many of her friends into Shellie's life.

Though the school year had barely begun, there were constant reminders that this was the last year for a third of the student body. Senior pictures, ordering class rings and graduation announcements all seem to intensify the feelings of conclusiveness. All of this was going on in concert with one of the most important aspects of high school life: football!

Having been one of the highlights of my high school career, I could vividly remember my senior year of play. Knowing that this was the last season, the last homecoming, and eventually the last game, intensified every emotion related to it.

Each week seemed to begin and end on Friday as we progressed through the season of home and away games. As homecoming approached, Amanda had been asked to the dance, and concerns were mounting as each day passed because of no invitation being offered to Shellie.

Now only slightly more than a week remained before the big game. Ruth kept asking Amanda each afternoon if she had heard any more about someone asking Shellie to the dance, and more importantly, if the nominations for homecoming queen had been announced. Each day, Amanda would respond in the negative, and each day, Ruth would affirm her inner conviction that Shellie would not only be asked to the dance, but also be nominated. While not wanting to seem negative, I tried to mitigate any unrealistic optimism, but to no avail.

On the Thursday prior to homecoming week, I was working upstairs in the study when I heard the front door open and the familiar announcement as Shellie stepped into the entry, "Honey, I'm home." Though we had grown accustomed to this cheerful declaration each day, it never failed to lift our spirits and put a smile on our faces.

Within minutes, I heard Shellie bounding up the stairs and down the hallway toward the study, while at the same time preceding her entrance by shouting "Daddy" over and over again. Upon entering the room, her eyes were as wide as her smile as she approached the front of the desk.

"Look what I have," as she thrust a paper forward. Not having any idea what could involve so much enthusiasm, I inquired while reaching for the paper, "What is it."

"Read it and weep," she said, her face beaming with excitement. But before my eyes could focus on the words, she could no longer hold it back. "I've been nominated to be homecoming queen!"

"What?" I said with a joyful laugh in my voice as I reach for my reading glasses. As I began reading the single paragraph at the top of the page, I could hear Ruth coming down the hall at a much slower pace than Shellie had. By the time she entered the room, I had finished enough of the message to know that forty girls had been nominated on the first ballot, and that on the following Monday, the names listed below would be narrowed down to the ten finalists. Shellie's name was easy to location on the long list, as someone had caused it to stand out with the use of a yellow high-lighter.

Ruth was now standing directly behind Shellie with a condescending smile from ear to ear. As I looked above Shellie and into Ruth's eyes, I shook my head from side to side and said, "Well, it looks like I have egg on my face."

Shellie's eyebrows formed a quizzical frown, as she stated, "No you don't."

My focus dropped from Ruth to Shellie's puzzled face and I smiled and reassured her it was merely an expression. Looking back up at Ruth, we exchanged a private smile.

Though my heart was filled with joy and happiness for our sweet daughter, and while trying to express how proud we were of her, my mind involuntarily shifted to a more practical bias. Not fully realizing the poor timing of my good intentions, I invited Shellie to come around the desk and stand next to me. Taking a piece of paper, I quickly drew four rows containing ten small lines in each. I then began to explain, in very simple terms, the process of elimination, and had barely drawn a line around the bottom row of ten figures when I heard Ruth exhale an audible sound of disgust.

As I stopped and looked up at her, she profoundly expressed her thoughts without saying a word. *"Please... let her enjoy the moment!"* Realizing the error of my ways, I slowly turned back to Shellie and said as convincingly as possible, "And I think there is an excellent chance you will be one of these ten." Then I returned to Ruth for acceptance and she closed her eyes and smiled while nodding her head up and down.

Not really caring to fully understand the quiet dialogue that had just taken place, Shellie grabbed the piece of paper containing her name and ran from the office while shouting that she had to tell the rest of the family and most of all, Kathy Hansen, her closest and dearest friend.

I deferred turning my head until Ruth had begun walking toward the doorway. I knew, as sure as sunrise, that she could not leave without a parting statement. Pausing only momentarily at the door, she slowly swung her head around until our eyes met. In a sweet yet patronizing voice, she said with complete confidence, "I hate to tell you I told you so...but...I told you so."

As she continued down the hall, I openly laughed and dropped my head while whispering the words, "Women...you got t' love 'em."

Throughout the following weekend, the conversation continued with boundless optimism. I tried with full intent to join in the reverie, but my conservative nature caused an uneasy pessimism to undermine my inner confidence. More than anything, I wanted to enjoy the hopes and dreams of our precious daughter, but the fear of reality and disappointment pulled at my heart. A portion of that anxiety was eliminated Saturday night as Aaron McDonough asked Shellie to the homecoming dance. He was not only a wonderful young man, but also the son of our family orthodontist and president of the senior class. That evening, as we gathered around the dinner table, I looked over at Shellie and said, "So, you're going to the homecoming dance with the president of the senior class, huh?"

Shellie closed her eyes and tilted her head upwards as she mimicked the words from the Grey Poupon commercial, "But of course!" Laughter broke out around the room as several of us tried our imitation of those famous words.

On Monday afternoon, the 22nd of October, a scene unfolded with uncanny similarity to the one of the previous week. I was once again up in the study when I heard the front door fly open. There was no familiar cry of "Honey I'm home," but I could hear the footsteps racing up the stairs and running down the hall as if Shellie instinctively knew that's where I'd be. Bursting into the room and almost out of breath, she shouted, "I made it, I made it! I'm in the top ten! I'm a finalist!"

Her infectious excitement swept through my body like a wave. This time there was no thought of pessimism or cautious outlook. The glory of this moment was enough. As I hugged her and the tears welled up in my eyes, I allowed no negative thoughts to come near. She was one of ten girls selected out of a student body of more that fifteen hundred, and that was honor enough for anyone. By the time we had run down the hall and reached the top of the stairs, Ruth was at the landing. Through joyful tears, she repeated, "I knew it, I just knew it."

After the customary calls were made to "Nana and Bampa" and other members of the family, reality started to set in. There was a great deal to do in the three short days before the huge homecoming pep rally. The paper that Shellie had brought home detailed the rehearsal schedule, how the program would be carried out that night, and what the fathers should wear when they introduced their daughters at center court.

Amanda and Ruth made arrangements to look for another formal dress for Thursday night, and Kim Calton, another top ten finalist and neighbor, came over to ensure us that she would take Shellie to the rehearsals and bring back any information that we needed. Arrangements were made for Ruth's sister, Sharon, to fly out from California and all other routine activities seemed to pale in insignificance as pictures were taken, alterations were made, and schedules rearranged.

Finally, Thursday arrived and no sooner had Shellie gotten home from school than the flurry of activities started. The chaos was interrupted only for a short while, as Ruth had to leave for the airport to pick up her sister.

All the way there, the tears kept streaming down her face. Wiping them away only remedied the outward show of emotion temporarily. These were not tears brought on by a combination of causes, but by a singular secret that she had locked in her heart, a secret she had not allowed herself to share with anyone that day. The joy of seeing her sister would help to suppress its confidentiality. Upon returning home, the mayhem was quickly renewed.

Makeup and hair, nylons and shoes, this was "girls' stuff" in its finest hour; much like a wedding, when the best thing the guys can do is stay out of the wake turbulence.

With only a half hour to go before leaving for the school, much of the dust was beginning to settle. I was becoming as nervous as an expectant father as visions of disappointment once again invaded my thoughts. Would Shellie truly realize what an honor it was just to be one of the top ten finalists? How would she react when the queen was announced? Could she really understand the concept of being a gracious loser? My hopes were as high as anyone's, but my fears could not be denied. Alone, I paced back and forth in the living room until I heard the door open in Amanda's room at the top of the stairs.

Slowly, Shellie descended each step and then turned to enter the living room. From the moment I first saw her, I failed to remember to breathe. She was in a beautiful white gown with a yellow sash. A purple banner cascaded off her shoulder with the words "Homecoming Queen Candidate 1997" emblazoned in silver sparkles. Her hair was done up on her head and the makeup was done to perfection. She was absolutely stunning and I knew she had to feel as beautiful as she looked. In words of quiet confidence, she asked, "Well, what do you think, Daddy?"

With barely enough air to form the words, I responded, "You take my breath away." Sensing my pride, she rushed to my arms, and while in her embrace, I opened my moistened eyes to look at Ruth and silently conveyed the message, *"Well done, well done."*

Once the emotions had settled down and everyone had regained their composure, Shellie and I had a few private moments in the living room to go over the agenda for the evening. While sitting in the wing-back chair next to the window, Shellie drew close to my side as we rehearsed the sequence of events and what each of us were to do. After Shellie reassured me that there was nothing to worry about, I had to concede that there was one more thing to discuss. Again, I had the paper and pencil ready, but this time the ten stick figures were already drawn.

Slowly, I began my presentation as to how there would be only one girl selected out of the ten to be the queen and how the others had to be very happy for that lucky person. Before I could continue, Shellie interrupted while pointing to the one I had circled. "That's me, I'm going to be the queen," she stated. My heart started to sink with fear as I continued the explanation about the first and second attendants. Once again she interrupted and reaffirmed her belief. I stopped just momentarily to try to conceive a different path to take. I had barely begun my new line of logic, when she interrupted me for the third time by saying, "But Daddy, I'm going to be the queen." My patience was now starting to run about as thin as my ability to convey my message, so I stopped abruptly and asked in a rather matter-of-fact voice, "Shellie, why do you think that you're going to be the queen?" While looking me straight in the eyes and with a tender smile, she softly said, "Because you always call me princess."

Her words had stopped me cold. All the normal insight that a parent usually receives to answer one of their children's questions or statements was gone. A number of convergent thoughts seemed to collide in my mind and each one was rejected. I couldn't say: "Just because I call you princess, it doesn't mean that you really are one." Nor would it be right to say: "Just because you're a princess to me, doesn't mean you're a princess to everyone." All I could do was to remember to start breathing again and admit defeat.

Shellie leaned forward and gave me a kiss on the cheek and turned to walk into the kitchen in total indifference to the fact that the world had just stopped for a moment.

As I sat there alone for a few minutes, a collage of thoughts seemed to overlay one another.

What's in a name, I wondered?

Shellie did not understand the mechanics of lying or deceit. She took things at face value in total trust. If I called her a princess, then that's what she was. And it's only logical that a princess becomes a queen. I remembered how, in some foreign cultures, the parents named their children after certain character traits, and in the majority of cases, that was just what the child became. It had even been true with Ruth's name, which meant "sweetness." To be ruthless, meant to be without sweetness. As my mind came back to the present moment, I smiled, and as I slowly shook my head from side to side and said under my breath, "I've got to watch what I say."

Although we arrived at the high school at least a half hour before Spartan Spectacular was scheduled to begin, the large parking lot was already half full. So that Shellie wouldn't have to walk outside any farther than necessary in a full-length white gown, I dropped her and the rest of the family off at the doors leading into the gymnasium. After parking the car, I had a moment to myself to reflect on the incredible events of this day. While sitting in the car and looking out toward the west, I could see the long beams of orange and yellow light emanating from behind the Oquirrh Mountains and stretching across the cloudless sky. Each time I witnessed this quiet yet awesome display of nature, it never failed to conjure up an image in my mind of the creation of the world. My first thought was to say a quick prayer in recognition of this beautiful sight and the emotions that filled my heart. But the majesty of nature spread out before me caused me not to want to close my eyes. Instead, I realized that a moment of private meditation would be equally accepted. Thoughts of thankfulness filled my mind: for a lovely wife and wonderful marriage, for four beautiful children and the opportunities they each have, and for an abundant and full life that I had only dreamt about twenty years ago. Twenty years...where had the time gone? Like the luminous tones that where cast across the sky, our life had been painted with a brush of many colors. Each child had brought a rainbow of emotions and experiences into our lives. But tonight the light would shine brightest on Shellie, her moment in the sun, which seemed to dispel any of the dark clouds of the past. *"Shellie will be all right, Shellie will be all right."* How I had misinterpreted the answer to a quiet prayer in a lonely jetway in San Francisco some eighteen years ago. It hadn't said,

"Shellie will not have Down syndrome." It merely stated, *"Don't worry, take comfort, I will watch after her; Shellie will be all right."* Watch after her, He had indeed, in a way that had exceeded all expectations. How curious it is that often times, things that first appear to be our biggest trials turn out to be some of our greatest blessings.

As the color in the evening sky continued to change, I was grateful for this private audience with nature I had been granted. If only momentarily, it had offered me a quiet reprieve from the nervous excitement of the day and helped to restore a proper perspective.

Entering through the large doors leading into the area outside the gymnasium, I was quickly brought back into the realities of the evening. Students, parents, football players, and cheerleaders all combined in a form of ordered chaos as they hurried toward their appropriate places. I quickly found our family sitting about half way up the stands, slightly left of center court. After taking my place next to Ruth, she handed me a copy of the program that detailed the events of the evening. There were nearly a dozen events that would take place leading up to the final announcement of the queen, each intended to build momentum up to the crowning point of the evening.

Well prior to the beginning of the program, the stands were full and an overflow crowd was now positioning into every available vantage point. The pep band had begun to play and already an air of excitement filled the arena. The presentation of the colors and the National Anthem only momentarily subdued the large assembly.

Directly across from us, on the opposite sideline of the basketball court, was a tall wooden podium with a single microphone. To the right of it were seated the school administrators and faculty advisors. To the left were an equal number of student body officers. At the end of the court, farthest from where we were sitting, was the football team in their numbered black jerseys. On the other end was the band that brought everyone to their feet as they played the school song. Following the welcome by the principal, Dee Jensen, and the introductions by the student body president, Leslie Allard, the program continued through musical numbers by various school groups and dance companies and by the cheerleaders initiating a rally through the entire audience. This all led up to where the coach introduced each football player by name and position to thunderous applause. It was during this part of the program that the fathers were to gather at the far right corner of the gym and the ten queen candidates were to assemble at the opposite corner of the court. While seeing several of the fathers beginning to leave the stands, I looked over at Ruth and raised my eyebrows and said, "Well, it's just about show time."

"Are you nervous or excited?" she asked.

With this question, my smile quickly changed to a more contemplative expression. I honestly wanted to evaluate my feelings as well as give Ruth an answer. "A little bit of both, I think. I only hope Shellie can understand what an exceptional life she has had and what an honor these incredible kids have given her just to be a candidate and included in this way."

"Shellie appreciates all of her friends, and one look in her face will tell you how much she enjoys life. Maybe we should learn to take each day with as much courage and grace as she does."

Once again, Ruth stated in a single sentence something that I would think about during the entire time it took me to leave the stands and find my position across the court. Courage and grace. What perfect words to describe Shellie's life.

As I stood there with the other fathers and looked back upon the hundreds of people assembled in this large arena, the noise of the crowd and announcement of the names were all but drowned out by my thoughts. In the quietness of my mind, I began to review a multitude of various scenes, each working their way backwards from the present moment: the vision of Shellie rushing into the study with the paper in her hand, the time when Amanda told her friends that if their plans didn't include Shellie, then she would rather not be included either, when Edward told me the people he liked most were the ones that treated Shellie the best, and the occasion where David left the dugout with baseball bat in hand to defend Shellie against a gang of older boys with a morbid concept of fun. Even those times when Ruth and I had to explain things to teachers and leaders about feelings and sensitivity that they could have learned by watching others far younger than themselves. But even the visions of waiting in the hall to find out if she had AIDS, or of Shellie lying in her hospital bed following the stroke, or of the operation at Stanford began to fade as my mind reverted once again toward the present. I felt as though a cool breeze had swept over me. Images returned of Shellie riding horses with her cousin Debbie and playing basketball with cheering friends, of Brett Kitchen, kneeling down in front of her, or of James Garrett taking her to a Hawaiian theme dance.

The uplifting experiences had far outnumbered any painful memories, and the life of a little princess, lived with courage and grace, had rewarded us all.

As my daydream faded back into the realities of the moment, the noise in the gymnasium returned to full intensity. The last of the football players had just been announced and it was now time for the presentation of the candidates. While hoping that my explanation in the living room earlier that evening had made some impression on Shellie, I had no idea of the lesson I was about to learn regarding winning and losing.

The noise in the auditorium provided an acceptable excuse for the lack of conversation between the ten of us, anxiously awaiting the beginning of the final event of the evening. With all of us dressed in similar dark-colored suits with a flower pinned to the left lapel, we must have looked like some paternal gathering of nervous fathers waiting to give our daughters away at some mass wedding ceremony.

Suddenly, the voice of the student body president echoed through the gymnasium speakers. "Ladies and gentlemen, we will now have the presentation of the ten final candidates for the 1997 Murray High Homecoming Queen." Cheers, applause, and a few "cat calls" from spirited students followed the announcement.

"In alphabetical order, our first candidate is, Miss Holly Babcock." Right on cue, both the father and daughter left the respective corners of the gym and proceeded to a point directly under opposite baskets. By that time, the applause had died down and the announcer continued with a biography containing information about what activities or groups this girl was involved in, along with her favorite food, most fun vacation, and most embarrassing moment. This presentation, if timed just right, was supposed to last throughout the sequence of the father and daughter walking toward each other until meeting at center court. There, the father would present his daughter with a bouquet of flowers, walk her forward to the edge of the court, and then down to a predetermined spot to the point where all ten girls would finally stand. The announcer would end the biography by once again stating the girl's name, upon which the father would return to his seat. It was reassuring to watch three presentations before it was Shellie's turn.

I could feel my pulse quicken as the announcer continued, "And now the fourth candidate... Miss Shellie Eyre."

What happened next not only surprised, but also overwhelmed me. As if on some prearranged signal, the entire audience rose to their feet and began a thunderous applause. In total amazement, I stood there trying to take in the significance of this special moment. The noise from clapping and cheering, along with students shouting her name, flooded my senses to the extent that I failed to move. Not until I noticed Shellie walking toward the center of the court did I realize that I had missed my cue. I hurried diagonally from the corner of the court to a point on the center line where Shellie had progressed.

The standing ovation continued as we met at center court and I handed her the bouquet of flowers. Bending down, I gave her a kiss on the cheek and asked", "What do you think of this?"

Through a radiant smile, she simply replied, "I think it's great." We then proceeded straight forward to the edge of the court and stopped only momentarily before turning to the left and continuing to our predetermined spot.

By this time, the applause had begun to die down, and before leaving the court, I whispered in her ear, "Good luck, Princess," to which I received a loving and confident reply: "Thanks, Daddy."

As I walked off the basketball floor, I could hear the beginning of the brief biography of Shellie's life that was supposed to accompany our promenade onto the court.

While alone in the tunnel beneath the stadium seats, I stopped and leaned my back up against the wall. Quickly, I tried to rehearse and relive the experience I had just shared with our daughter and hundreds of others.

The announcement of the following girl's name, the applause and the beginning of her personal narrative, drew my attention back to the doors I had just passed through. Closing my eyes, I could vividly recreate the scene taking place just a few yards away. All those beautiful young girls were standing in a line with a common hope in their hearts to be named homecoming queen. A moment many of them had dreamed about for years was now only minutes away.

But there was one among them whose understanding of this singular event was much more recent. One, whose goals and aspirations had always been more near term, and whose comprehension of the distant future was more compressed.

In a fruitless attempt to gain a more personal appreciation for what Shellie was experiencing, I stood there, trying to recall similar experiences I had enjoyed in my past. All seemed insignificant to the importance this would have on her life and the impact it would have on others.

As I heard the next candidate announced, I became aware of the amount of time I had been leaning against the wall. Though I savored the solitude that the passageway had provided, I knew I had to return to my family before my absence was questioned.

Upon taking my place next to Ruth, she slowly turned to me and softly inquired, "Well, what did you think of that?" As our eyes met, she could tell that the absence of a reply was the result of too many emotions too near the surface and a lack of words to adequately express them. Her quiet reminder of the overwhelming reception afforded our daughter brought with it the first admission that tonight could be more wonderful than I had previously allowed myself to consider.

At the conclusion of the presentation of the final candidate, a strange silence returned to the auditorium. As all ten girls stood facing the audience, each one in resplendent beauty, the clear and stead voice of Leslie Allard echoed through the speakers. "The second attendant is...Bricannie Towers." The ensuing applause tended to validate my feelings of this wonderful girl. Her younger sister, McCall, had been Shellie's best friend in their special education class. Bricannie had always treated Shellie and McCall and everyone else with sincere and selfless affection. I had witnessed in her the same humbling effect I had seen in our own children in having a handicapped sibling. There comes with it a compassion and tenderheartedness that cannot be taught by parents.

Many years ago, I had silently wondered how Shellie's condition would affect our other children. Now, as I looked into the smiling face of Bricannie Towers, I was reminded of those sitting right next to me and the powerful and positive influence it had made in their lives.

Once again, the voice over the loudspeakers brought us back to a continuance of the evening. "The first attendant is...April Perschon." I had been holding my breath in hopes that I would hear Shellie's name, but this announcement brought with it a shower of differing emotions. April was a beautiful and active little girl when, at the age of ten, she was struck with a severe brain tumor that would alter her course in life. Her enduring sense of humor had captivated the hearts of all who knew her. I had missed her standing ovation while I was outside of the auditorium, but I was very aware of the incredible heart of this student body.

As proud as I was, my selfish side could not help but do the math. It had come down to a one in eight chances. Quickly, my mind raced through the various reasons for and the possible outcomes of the final announcement.

My eyes were tightly closed as I heard, "We would now like to introduce last year's Homecoming Queen, Crystal Kerr, who will crown this year's lucky queen." Although I had opened my eyes and clapped along with the others, I could hardly raise my head for fear of interrupting the myriad of thoughts going through my mind. Involuntarily, as if to aid my concentration, my eyes closed again as the now familiar voice began, "And now we would like to present to you the Murray High School Homecoming Queen for 1997...Miss Shellie Eyre!"

For a moment, I was stunned. I honestly couldn't tell if I had shouted her name in my mind or if I had actually heard it with my ears. The eruption of noise around me quickly confirmed the latter. As everyone rose to their feet, and I sat there for just a moment in quiet reflection of this remarkable event. Silent prayers for a little girl had just been answered, and hopes and dreams and expectations had been exceeded. My first thought was what this would mean to Shellie's life, but as I stood to join the others in a celebration of joy, I began to realize for the first time, what it meant to everyone in that room. As I saw the other candidates rush to gather around Shellie and the standing ovation and cheering continue in intensity, I started to understand how so many elements had come together at this moment.

My emotions were far too strong, and my ability to express them far too weak, to do anything more than to look at Ruth. A familiar, confident, and dauntless smile radiated from her face, but it was the mischievous wink that betrayed her secret. My eyes widened as I stared at her and exclaimed, "You knew, didn't you!"

Any condescending expression had left her face and was replaced with tender compassion as she whispered. "All day long, and that's my gift to you."

I questioned if I had the capacity to appropriately appreciate all of my blessings. I wanted very much to fully comprehend and enjoy each individual emotion.

By now, many of us were making our way down the stands toward the basketball floor below. From there, we continued to the circle of friends and well wishers that had surrounded the radiant new queen. As we waited for our turn to hug and congratulate her, I noticed, out of the corner of my eye, a woman that was staring at me. She had her arm around the shoulders of a beautiful young lady, dressed in an elegant gown and holding the flowers that her father had presented to her just moments ago. Realizing I didn't know the name of the candidate, nor had I ever been introduced to her mother, I merely returned the pleasant smile she offered. But instead of just accepting the reciprocal gesture, she removed her arm from her daughter and walked toward me. I knew that she was going to say something to compliment or congratulate Shellie and I was mentally preparing what I hoped would be an appropriate and sincere acknowledgement. But as she approached me, I was completely unprepared for what she said. Without introducing herself, she graciously stated. "Every girl, who ever wanted to be homecoming queen, got to be one tonight. There were no losers this evening."

Her unexpected statement left me standing there motionless for the time it took her to return to her daughter.

That was it! That was what I had been trying to understand about everyone else's reaction to the overwhelming events of the evening. The idea that no one was a loser implied that everyone was a participant. It made no difference if you were a student, a teacher, or a parent; everyone had won. We had all been associated with and participated in an experience that made us proud of our children, our school, our community, and ourselves. Once again, we had renewed that submerged affirmation that we were all okay, that society, with all of its selfish interests, was still basically good. We left the auditorium that evening not only with thankfulness in our hearts, but as more complete human beings.

The following morning, we opened the paper to find a huge picture of Shellie, surrounded by all the other candidates, on the front page. Thousands around Salt Lake City and throughout Utah, now shared a story that had been experienced by just a few hundred.

During the day, as preparations were being made for the big homecoming game, we received numerous phone calls in recognition of the previous night. Shellie could not only enjoy the game as a Spartan Pepper, but just before half time, she would change her Spartan Peppers uniform for a formal gown. As the final moments of the first half came to a close, in the back of the Snack Shack, Ruth had once again transformed Shellie into a queen. We then made our way around the darkened track to the waiting convertibles on the opposite side of the field. As I was helping Shellie into the back seat of the shiny new car to where she would sit on the back deck, I heard a voice exclaim from the opposing team stands, "There she is, there's the girl in the newspaper." Once again, I stood in awe as the rival team fans stood and applauded as she passed by. The three cars made their way around to the much larger home-team stands where the crowd and the noise erupted. There were television news reporters and newspaper photographers running backwards to catch the images of this evening's royal court and the exuberant supporters. I could only imagine what was going through Shellie's mind. Impressions and memories were being made that would last a lifetime, many that could be reviewed and enjoyed over and over again in pictures and video tape.

Following the game, unfortunately lost by six points, we rushed home to see the events on the evening news. With Shellie sitting directly in front of the television and surrounded by family and friends, we quickly switched from the various local channels in order not to miss each presentation. What followed was one of the most poignant and revealing moments in Shellie's life.

We were all silently glued to the screen as the anchorman for one of the network affiliates began to introduce the story. Before turning it over to the local reporter, he began with a background of Shellie's life. Toward the end of the introduction he stated, "The Homecoming Queen of Murray High School was born with Down syndrome.

Slowly, Shellie rose up on her knees and turned to look at Ruth, sitting on the couch just slightly to her right and behind her. It seemed as if the voices from the television had been temporarily muted as she stated in questioned disbelief, "I have Down syndrome?"

The question hung in the air for what seemed like minutes, and now with all eyes focused on Ruth, she tenderly replied, "Yes, sweetheart...you do." We had never told Shellie that she was born with this infirmity. We had never acknowledged to her that there was any difference between her and anyone else in our family. Like all of our other children, she had been encouraged to participate in whatever worthwhile activity she desired. In everything, competitive horseback riding, modeling, league basketball, she had been accepted by all and rewarded like few others.

It was obvious to each of us that the realization of this newly discovered truth was sinking into her mind as she turned her attention once again to the images on the screen.

Shouts of "There she is," and recognition of other familiar faces brought the return of joyful voices around the room. Another television channel showed a variation of the now familiar scene and another reminder of what made this event so very special.

Following the news and due to the lateness of the hour, friends made their way home and preparations were made for each of us to enjoy a good night's rest. After all, this was not over yet. Tomorrow night was the homecoming dance with all of its anticipated excitement and associated pageantry.

With the formal now safely hung in the closet and Shellie in her warm pajamas, she crawled into bed. Before her prayers were said I took a moment to look around her room and quietly reflect on the visual representations of an exceptional life. A number of Special Olympic medals were displayed above her bed. Numerous pictures of her with her dates while attending the dances over the last year and a half were positioned around the room. A poster of Brad Pitt hung behind the door, and on the middle of the dresser was the crown of a homecoming queen.

What a wonderfully normal, and at the same time, incredibly exceptional high school experience she had enjoyed. The monogram of this room was one of a life lived with courage and grace, dignity and hope. Never in my wildest dreams could I have envisioned seventeen years ago what I beheld with my eyes and felt in my heart that night.

Following a prayer, filled with reverent appreciation for the events of the last two days, I kissed Shellie good night and turned to walk from the room. Just before reaching the door, Shellie quietly inquired, "Daddy, just one more thing.

What does it mean to be handicapped? What does it mean that I'm handicapped?"

This was no question with a short or perfunctory answer. It was one that could not be addressed from my position at the door, but required and rightfully deserved, a return to her bedside. It was easy to discern from the look in her eyes that this was a question from her heart and deserved the honesty with which it was asked. I could only hope that my words would be directed from resources outside of myself.

"Everyone has disabilities, sweetheart. I have had several operations on my knee, so I can no longer play football, and it hurts me to play racquetball or handball, but I can still enjoy running and lots of other sports. Your grandmother didn't have perfect hearing, so she had to wear a hearing aid, but that didn't keep her from doing anything she wanted to do in the church or at clubs or anywhere else. When you were a little girl you were sick with what is called a stroke, and you know it made your left leg and arm much weaker than those on your right side. But as serious as it was, it hasn't kept you from playing the guitar or dancing or all the other things you love to do. So what does it mean that you have a handicap? It means that you are just like everyone else, but that your handicaps are different from mine or grandma's and many other people's. The fact that you have Down syndrome might make it more difficult for you to do a number of things, but if you keep that wonderful spirit in your heart, the Lord will enable you to do just about anything you want. Remember, we all might have handicaps, but we just can't let those handicaps have us."

I paused for a moment to get Shellie's reaction to what I had just said. I thought I would be able to tell by the expression on her face if my sincere attempt could do justice to the importance of her question. Within a very short moment, a smile came over her face, and with an indication of total trust, her eyes sparkled again as she simply replied, "Okay... Thanks, Daddy...Good night." I left the room wishing I could accept my trials and weaknesses with such powerful faith.

The next day was once again filled with the activities and vexations of transforming two already beautiful girls into two even more beautiful girls. My role was once again to stay out of the way. I took great solace in knowing that this cacophony of disorganized confusion was taking place at countless other homes and ending with the same results: a father, standing in awe and wonder as his daughter asks, "Well, what do you think, Daddy?"

That evening, on the ten o'clock news, we watched Shellie for the third consecutive night, as the story continued to be reported from the homecoming dance.

A story we thought would end that night has continued to the present writing of this book. It has been retold in talks and speeches, in syndicated newspaper articles and national magazines, and discussed by producers and writers. It is not only a tribute to a sweet little girl, but equally as much of a tribute to a high school student body who were much more concerned about the feelings of others than they were about their tan lines. It's also a tribute to the girls who had anticipated for years the thought of becoming Homecoming Queen, and then, on the day that their dreams might be fulfilled, had decided to vote for someone else, someone they wanted to be Homecoming Queen more than they wanted it for themselves. This type of unselfishness is seldom seen in mature adults, never mind in a whole student body of aspiring young men and women.

It was their acts and deeds and the teaching of their parents and the leadership of caring administrators and teachers that was being celebrated over and over again. To paraphrase a newspaper quote by one of the vice principals of the school, Glo Merrill said, "Tonight, you have seen that the students voted on inner beauty...and this election is a testament to the value of including students with disabilities into mainstream classes." We can only hope that every student body would look for its Shellie Eyre, and that every Shellie Eyre could be blessed with such a student body.

Seven months later, with her family and grandparents proudly watching from front row seats in the balcony of the same auditorium where it all began, the superintendent of schools announced Shellie's name. As she walked across the stage, with her ever-present limp being eclipsed by her boundless smile, to receive her high school completion certificate, once again, on an inward cue, 1429 students came to their feet at the same time. Their continuing example was only then, emulated by those of us sitting in the stands. The ovation lasted until she had waved to everyone and had left the stage.

My thoughts drifted back to that poignant question asked from her bedside some seven months ago, "Daddy, what does it mean to be handicapped?" A very dear friend once told me of the origin of that word. Many decades ago, it was thought that a person born with these disabilities would be useless to society. Once they were old enough, they were told to stand in the street with their *cap* in their *hand* and beg for offerings. Our picture of Shellie could not have been further from this representation. Tonight, she had completed one of the many accomplishments we had envisioned in her life. Rather than sadly standing with her cap in her hand, she was proudly walking in her cap and gown. Instead of accepting handouts from others, she had given more to us that we could ever repay.

As I stood there, clapping with several thousand people, I looked down at the ordered rows of enthusiastic graduates. Recently, there had been a great deal of media coverage given to a few disturbed and troubled individuals who had brought violence and suffering to their communities and schools. But throughout this country, on such a graduation night, were tens of thousands of students who had gone to school, attended their classes, and completed their work. They might not have made the evening news, but they were the ones who would make history.

When the last name was called, and with the words, "Ladies and gentlemen, I present to you the class of 1998," a burst of caps flew into the air. For just a brief second, they froze there, and I knew then, that the world had just become a better place.

TEN

Past, Present, and Distant Future

From the first day I began writing this book, well over a year ago, I have looked forward to this chapter, not because it is the last, but because if affords me the opportunity to share the feelings of my heart with my family and anyone else who might read it. Probably more than any other event in my life, Shellie's birth caused me to begin a life-long search for answers to eternal questions. The lessons I have been taught and the paths that have guided me to a personal knowledge and a conviction of my beliefs are something very precious and dear to me.

In a limited quest to understand why Shellie came to this earth with so many challenges, what her role in this life and our family was going to be, and what would be her everlasting consequences and rewards, I have been blessed with a broader comprehension and appreciation for my own mortality.

I have come to learn of the battles she must have fought and won before she was even born. Only one fourth of the children conceived with Down syndrome survive the entire pregnancy and are not miscarried or spontaneously aborted. This was evidence to me that Shellie had a unique and distinctive mission in life and that I had, not the obligation, but the opportunity to be a part of it.

At first, my search was a combination of gathering medical facts and spiritual insights. But because of my limited abilities in the former, over the years a much greater effort has been put forth in trying to comprehend things outside the physical disciplines. I greatly appreciate those who dedicate their talents and abilities in genetic research and medical studies, but by necessity, my goals were much more immediate.

I have come to understand that adversity is not only something that strengthens us, but is part of the privilege of being human. In the privacy of a darkened jetway many years ago, I begged for the Lord to change Shellie. What I received was a gift from Someone with infinite knowledge and an eternal perspective; He had changed me instead.

I had always found great comfort in going to Him and in acknowledging His hand in all aspects of my life. Though we may be the one who tosses the coin, it is the Lord who determines how it will fall. And if He truly directs our every step, then why should we question what happens along the way? In trying to better understand why Shellie had to suffer at different times in her life, it only felt appropriate to go to Someone who had suffered more than any of us could ever comprehend.

My search began in a very logical and methodical way. I wanted desperately to know of our premortal state. I knew better than to think that the events leading up to our birth were designless or chaotic, that they, like all other elements of the universe were purposeful, orderly, and part of a divine plan. I have come to believe, with all my heart, that because of the type of individual she was in the premortal world, Shellie was given the opportunity to come to earth with this infirmity, that she might be protected from some of the temptations and responsibilities of this life in order that she could return to be with Him forever. I maintain that she made this choice with her own free will, and words cannot express how much I respect her for it. I feel that there is a very good chance in the premortal sphere that we chose our family order. That being the case, I know I would have chosen her, and I am humbled and honored that she chose me. I will be forever grateful that Ruth and I and our children will be an eternal family unit. I can only hope that we can live the type of life to be deserving of these blessings.

I believe that, while we are on this earth, much of how we view and experience life is dependent, not only on our actions, but by our perspectives and attitudes. I am required by my profession to be away from my family a good deal of time. This used to bother me much more than it does now, not because the circumstances have changed, but because I perceive it from a revised viewpoint. I now know that Ruth and I have become one, one in purpose and one in eternal goals. Therefore, when we are apart it helps me to remember that, in forever, there is no such thing as time, and in infinity, there is no such thing as distance. Accordingly, we are always with each other regardless of the physical distance between us.

Shellie has been blessed with this optimistic outlook her entire life. Each day is filled with exciting experiences and wondrous discoveries. What parents wouldn't give this gift to their child if they could? Fortunately, Shellie's heavenly parents did. Ever since I have come to understand this special interrelationship, I have stepped out from underneath a self-imposed dark cloud and have enjoyed living in the shadow of her light. Many other lives have been illuminated by the knowledge of her story, and many burdens have been lightened. I found myself coming to an understanding of her past, an appreciation of the present, and a comprehension of her distant future.

In regards to thoughts of these three distinctive phases of life, Oliver Wendell Holmes once said, "What lies behind us and what lies before us are tiny matters compared to what lies within us." But what lies within us is our spirit, made up of celestial material, which existed long before we were here and will continue forever. It cannot be altered by birth defects, or accidents, or illnesses, only by how we think, feel, and understand, and those alterations of the spirit can be eternal in nature.

Possibly, because of the pessimistic outlook we received from doctors long ago, and from seriously outdated material, I have lived for many years with the possibility that Shellie would precede me into the next life. As a result, I have tried to come to an understanding of the hereafter.

I have read with considerable interest, many stories about individuals who have shared an experience beyond this life. I have been surprised and reassured at the similarities that exist in each account. But once again, the majority of my personal insight has come from scripture study and prayer. I believe with all my heart in a post-mortal life, and I look forward to one special event more than anything else I can comprehend in my distant future. It has been the source of a reoccurring dream over the past several years. And though it is but a dream today, I know by the power of a personal testimony that the day will come when it will be a reality.

Within its images, I can envision a time when I will pass from this world and be escorted into the next. The vision of she who will greet me overwhelms my senses. Straining forward to see into the brilliant light, I can discern, with increasing clarity, the perfect form of a beautiful woman. Her graceful walk towards me is no longer encumbered by an impaired leg and she is tall in stature and elegant in movement. I can now see her resplendent face and radiant smile, with features no longer affected by imperfect genes.

A feeling of indescribable peace sweeps over me, yet my emotions will only allow a single acknowledgment: "Hello, Princess."

With hands and arms of identical size and perfect form, she reaches out to greet me. In an eloquent voice and with flawless diction, she imparts, "Welcome home, Dad."

How do I know with such complete certainty that I will see her in a perfect form, that we will all be together in a place with no more hunger or fear or pain? Because Heaven...would not be Heaven...if it were any other way.

The End

Acknowledgments

More than any other person I would like to thank my wife, Ruth, for her loving and patient support in every aspect of my life. All that I have that is of worth, is because of her. I continue to appreciate the opportunity we have to be eternal companions. I often wonder if that will be long enough,

To our children for their unselfish enjoyment of Shellie's moment in the sun.

To the students of Murray High School in Murray, Utah, for their genuine example of compassion and selflessness, and to their parents for raising them with such values.

To Elizabeth Wood for sharing with me her special insights and for her sincere compassion for others.

To Bob Turney for his encouragement to have this work published and to Jeff Lambson for making it possible.

*****

There are many others whose efforts have made Shellie's exceptional life possible. We would like to thank all those who initiated and supported the American Disabilities Act and Public Law 94-142. Its implementation has enriched the lives of the disabled, and through their inclusion, provided by its terms, they have influenced the hearts and minds of millions of others.

We would also like to acknowledge all the special education teachers who have dedicated their professional lives, time and talents, to the benefit of handicapped - children. You have given much more of yourselves than merely your knowledge and we hope you realize how much we appreciate all that you do.

*****

Finally, I would like to thank Shellie for the impact you have had on this family and many others who you might not even know. You willingly accepted your calling in life to teach us, through your gracious spirit, the lessons of patience, gratitude, faith, and unrestricted love. Our greatest joy comes in the knowledge that your influence will be everlasting and that your rewards will be literally...out of this world.

Notes

1. In 1866 John Langdon Down published an essay in England in which he described a set of children with common features who were distinct from other children with mental retardation. He referred to them a "Mongoloids." Dr. Down based this unfortunate name on his notion that these children looked like people from Mongolia. This ethnic insult came under fire in the early 1960's from Asian genetic researchers, and the term was dropped from scientific use. Instead, the condition became referred to as "Down's syndrome."

2. In the 1970's, an American revision of scientific terms changed the term from Down's syndrome to simply Down syndrome. It is still called Down's syndrome in the UK and some European countries.
Len Leshin, M.D., F.A.A.P.
Down Syndrome: Health Issues
http://www.ds-health.com

3. Dr. Middleton is a fictitious name and has been changed to protect the privacy of the individual with whom we had our first contact for genetic counseling.

4. Emily Perl Kingsley is a writer who joined the Sesame Street team in 1970 and has been writing for the show ever since. In 1987 she wrote, "Welcome to Holland." Emily Kingsley has written over 20 children's books and two Sesame Street home videos. She has won 12 Daytime Emmys and 9 nominations through

her work with Sesame Street along with numerous other awards with Easter Seals and the National Theatre of the Deaf.

5. Dr. Morris is a fictitious name and should not be associated with any practicing physician in the Seattle area at that time.

Shellie's family

from left to right: Ed, Shellie, Ruth, David, Ted, Amanda

About the Author

Ted Eyre was born and raised in Wyoming. Following graduation from Cheyenne East High School, he attended college at Brigham Young Univeristy and in Southern California. After a tour of duty in Viet Nam he returned to California to resume his flying career and there he met and married Ruth Ann Peters. They raised their four children in Murray, Utah and much of their family's story is contained in this book.

For further information about Shellie's Story or for specialty book orders or requests, please write to:

www.tedeyre@gmail.com